W0111178

Social Media and e-Diplomacy in China

Ying Jiang

Social Media and e-Diplomacy in China

Scrutinizing the Power of Weibo

Ying Jiang
Department of Media, Faculty of Arts
University of Adelaide
Adelaide
Australia

ISBN 978-1-137-59664-2   ISBN 978-1-137-59358-0   (eBook)
DOI 10.1057/978-1-137-59358-0

Library of Congress Control Number: 2017939885

© The Editor(s) (if applicable) and The Author(s) 2017
This work is subject to copyright. All rights are solely and exclusively licensed by the Publisher, whether the whole or part of the material is concerned, specifically the rights of translation, reprinting, reuse of illustrations, recitation, broadcasting, reproduction on microfilms or in any other physical way, and transmission or information storage and retrieval, electronic adaptation, computer software, or by similar or dissimilar methodology now known or hereafter developed.
The use of general descriptive names, registered names, trademarks, service marks, etc. in this publication does not imply, even in the absence of a specific statement, that such names are exempt from the relevant protective laws and regulations and therefore free for general use.
The publisher, the authors and the editors are safe to assume that the advice and information in this book are believed to be true and accurate at the date of publication. Neither the publisher nor the authors or the editors give a warranty, express or implied, with respect to the material contained herein or for any errors or omissions that may have been made. The publisher remains neutral with regard to jurisdictional claims in published maps and institutional affiliations.

Cover illustration: Pattern adapted from an Indian cotton print produced in the 19th century

Printed on acid-free paper

This Palgrave Pivot imprint is published by Springer Nature
The registered company is Nature America Inc.
The registered company address is: 1 New York Plaza, New York, NY 10004, U.S.A.

CONTENTS

LIST OF FIGURES

LIST OF TABLES

ABSTRACT

Public diplomatic communication is transforming due to the boom of social media. There are more than 165 foreign governmental organizations in China that have embarked on the use of Weibo (a hybrid of Facebook and Twitter in China) to engage with Chinese citizens. Journalists and a handful of scholars in China started paying attention to foreign embassies' use of Weibo; however, there has been no systematic study of the effectiveness and challenges of using Weibo for public diplomatic communication. Importantly, when it comes to incidents like the "Kunming terror attack" in China in March 2014, Chinese Weibo users tend to express severe nationalistic sentiments towards foreign countries' statements, and those Weibo accounts of foreign embassies became targets. Those nationalistic comments left on foreign embassies' Weibo pages, mainly criticizing those embassies' "soft statements," have caused the difficulties of e-diplomacy and are calling for immediate attention (Wu 2014).

This book, based on systematic research of Weibo usage by embassies in China from September 2015 to March 2016, *is the first in the academia* to explore the challenges that the use of Chinese Weibo (and Chinese social media in general) posed for foreign embassies, and to provoke thoughts about better ways to use these or other tools. It is not intended as an argument against the use of local popular social media for public diplomacy purposes, but to encourage a critical look at its practice and encourage those employing it to better analyze it.

This book doesn't deny that social media provides the right channel to reach youth populations, which is one of the major goals of current public diplomacy efforts. Weibo does give embassies a great channel to listen to and understand China's young populations' thoughts, aspirations, information seeking, and other behaviors. But when it comes to using the spaces for interaction, increased engagement, and thus furthering the goals of public diplomacy, the power of Weibo might have been overestimated.

REFERENCE

Wu. Y.S., (2014). *China's Media and Public Diplomacy: Illustrations from South Africa*. Paper presented atthe international conference China and Africa Media, Communications and Public Diplomacy.

PART I

Social Media Landscape Differences Between China and the West

CHAPTER 1

Introduction and Background Knowledge

Abstract Draws out the sketch of what the "problem" this thesis is dealing with, and clarifies the fundamental question this thesis examines: Is China's cyber-nationalism bringing any challenges to foreign embassies' practice of e-diplomacy in China? If it is, what sort of challenges is cyber-nationalism bringing to e-diplomacy?

Keywords Social media · China · Public relations
Political communication · Weibo · Public diplomacy

1.1 AIMS OF THE RESEARCH

The 2014 Kunming attack was a terrorist attack in the Chinese city of Kunming, Yunnan, on 1 March 2014. The incident, targeted against civilians, left 29 civilians and 4 perpetrators dead with more than 140 others injured. The attack has been called a "massacre" by some news media. On 2 March 2014, the US Embassy made a post on its Weibo account, stated: America condemns this horrible and senseless violence in Kunming. We send our sympathy to the families who lost their loved ones, and send our regard to everyone who is affected by this tragedy. Not long after this post, Chinese netizens expressed severe condemnation at the wording of this particular post, arguing that the use of "senseless violence" in the post demonstrates the US avoided considering this tragedy as a "terrorist attack". The US embassies' Weibo account has soon become a target

© The Author(s) 2017
Y. Jiang, *Social Media and e-Diplomacy in China*,
DOI 10.1057/978-1-137-59358-0_1

for Chinese Weibo users. It received more than 50,000 comments and 40,000 retweets; most of them were focusing on interrogating the avoidance of using "terrorist attack" by US Embassy in this statement.

Public diplomatic communication is transforming due to the boom of social media. There are more than 165 foreign governmental organizations in China that have embarked on the use of Weibo (a hybrid of Facebook and Twitter in China) to engage with Chinese citizens (ChinaLabs 2013a, b). Journalists and a handful of scholars in China started paying attention to foreign embassies' use of Weibo (ChinaLabs 2013a, b); however, there has been no systematic study of the effectiveness and challenges of using Weibo for public diplomatic communication. Importantly, when it comes to incidents like the "Kunming terror attack" in China in March 2014, Chinese Weibo users tend to express severe nationalistic sentiments towards foreign countries' statements, and those Weibo accounts of foreign embassies become targets. Those nationalistic comments left on foreign embassies' Weibo pages, mainly criticizing those embassies' "soft statements," have caused the difficulties of e-diplomacy and are calling for immediate attention.

This research, based on systemic research of Weibo usage by embassies in China from September 2014 to March 2015, is the first in the academia to explore the challenges that the use of Chinese Weibo (and Chinese social media in general) posed for foreign embassies, and to provoke thoughts about better ways to use these or other tools. It is not intended as an argument against the use of local popular social media for public diplomacy purposes, but to encourage a critical look at its practice and encourage those employing it to better analyze it. This book doesn't deny that social media provides the right channel to reach youth populations, which is one of the major goals of current public diplomacy efforts. Weibo does give embassies a great channel to listen to and understand China's young populations' thoughts, aspirations, information seeking, and other behaviors. But when it comes to using the spaces for interaction, increased engagement, and thus furthering the goals of public diplomacy, the power of Weibo might have been overestimated.

1.2   Key Terms in Use in This Book

There are issues of definitions in this thesis that are important to clarify. The first is "Weibo." Weibo is a Chinese microblogging (Weibo) website, in use by well over 30% of the world's Internet users, with a similar market penetration that Twitter has established in the USA. According to CNNIC (China Internet Network Information Center) report in 2015, there are 668 million Internet users, 594 million mobile Internet users, and 212 million monthly active Weibo users (CNNIC 2015). Although this most recent report did not mention the number of registered Weibo users, the CNNIC report in December 2012 announced that there are 309 million registered Weibo users in China (CNNIC 2013); the announced numbers of Weibo users provided by each Weibo service providers are much higher than the figure this official report disclosed. This is probably due to the competition between each Weibo service providers, but scholars and journalists in China often use the estimation of more than 400 million, which is somewhere between CNNIC's official report and commercial Weibo service providers' statistics.

It is important to note that, when Chinese people say "Weibo," it is commonly referred to Sina Weibo. However, Sina Weibo is just one of the various Weibo service competitors. Sina Weibo claims it has around 500 million registered accounts as of December 2012 (Gao 2013). Others include Tencent (the owner of QQ.com) which also alleged having a microblog site with 400 million registered accounts; and Sohu Weibo with over 100 million registered accounts. Therefore, it is more accurate to say "Tencent Weibo (Tenxun Weibo)" and "Sohu Weibo (Souhu Weibo)" to differentiate from "Sina Weibo (Xinlang Weibo)".

Due to its success of overseas users' penetration, Sina Weibo is still the most well-known Weibo service; therefore, the term Weibo used in this article refers to Sina Weibo.

"Public diplomacy 2.0," public diplomacy is a "term to describe the efforts by nations to win support and a favorable image among the general public of other countries, usually by way of news management and carefully planned initiatives designed to foster positive impressions" (Comor and Bean 2012, p. 204). The Internet has created an international space where communities around the world are more connected than ever. With this new level of interconnectivity, it is imperative that government utilize the tools provided by new media to communicate with foreign publics (Harris 2013). The innovation occurring in media has produced numerous social media tools worldwide. Rising numbers of additional users also contribute to social media's usefulness as a tool of public diplomacy (Mor 2012).

But a clear-cut definition of "public diplomacy 2.0" is not available; Cull (2010) from Harvard University summarized the three key characteristics of it: the first characteristic is the capacity of the technology to facilitate the creation of relationships around social networks and online communities. The second characteristic is the related dependence of Public Diplomacy 2.0 on user-generated content from feedback and blog comments to complex user-generated items such as videos or mash-ups. The third characteristic is the underlying sense of the technology as being fundamentally about horizontally arranged networks of exchange rather than the vertically arrange networks of distribution down which information cascaded in the 1.0 era. Cull has also pointed out that while the technology is entirely new, the underlying pattern of relationships underlying the operation of Public Diplomacy 2.0 is not.

"E-diplomacy," the term "e-diplomacy" describes new methods and modes of conducting diplomacy and international relations with the help of the Internet and information and communication technologies (ICTs). The term also refers to the study of the impact of these tools on contemporary diplomatic practices. E-diplomacy may be considered a subset of e-governance. Related (and interchangeable) terms include cyber diplomacy, net diplomacy, and digital diplomacy. E-Diplomacy as a form of public diplomacy has generated significant attention and criticism, with views ranging from technology allowing "people around the world to obtain ever more information through horizontal peer-to-peer networks rather than through the old vertical process by which information flowed down from the traditional sources of media authority" (Cull 2013) to claiming that efforts in public diplomacy often are understood as little more than top-down dissemination of (counter)-propaganda (Hoffman 2002).

Researcher Hanson from the Lowy Institute in Australia who had undertaken extensive research into the emerging role of e-diplomacy at the US State Department (Parliament of Australia 2012). Hanson commented that e-diplomacy was more than the use of either social media or public diplomacy:

> … e-diplomacy is not just about diplomats getting on Facebook and Twitter and promoting government messages; most of it is invisible to the public.

1.3   THE NATIONALISTIC SENTIMENTS

In November 2013, an anonymous post titled "You Are Nothing Without the Motherland" gradually gained momentum online. It has since been reposted by numerous Chinese media such as the Beijing

Daily and the Global times. The post used the "fallen-apart" Arabic Spring countries as examples to call for the Chinese people to stay alert for "Western anti-China powers," because the ultimate victim of "social instability" is the ordinary people (J.M. 2013). "A strong and stable motherland is the only way for the Chinese people to be happy and free," the article argued. It specifically called out the conspiracies by Western countries to bring down any potential rival. In particular, the USA "now lists China as its biggest threat." "Everybody knows that the US has been plotting to overthrow the rule of the Chinese Communities Party (CCP)" (Ibid).

According to the post, China will fall into chaos without the leadership of the Communist Party. The solution is to believe in Xi Jinping, China's current president who took power earlier this year. Because "Xi knows China and politics" due to his family background. More importantly, Xi has the courage to "fight tigers," i.e., fighting corruption.

Loving one's motherland is not only a Chinese phenomenon, but the point I make here is that this "love for the motherland" has been largely in the presentation of supporting the central government, despite the corruptions of local government which have been exposed in a lot of cases. The other presentation of "love for the motherland" is the resistance to critical comments towards China.

It is necessary to mention here that the anger towards the embassies described in this book is not expressed by all generations in China; it is a phenomenon concentrated amongst China's post 80s and 90s who have access to the Internet, and generally consume social media obsessively. According to Sina Weibo's 2015 report, 83% of their active users are between 17 and 33 years old (Sina Weibo 2015). They consume Western products such as Starbucks's coffee, or wearing Adidas shoes, getting Western degrees, and even becoming permanent residents of Western countries, the love for their motherland China is also getting stronger and stronger. They are proud of the accomplishments made by China.

Before foreign embassies opened up Weibo accounts, Chinese nationalists used to express their condemnation via website or their own blogs/ microblogs (Jiang 2012). Therefore, the appearance of foreign embassies' Weibo accounts provided a direct channel for condemnation, particularly when controversial events happen. It is interesting and worth investigating that even an embassy choose not to broadcast any political topics, and even Chinese followers are engaging with the embassy in a very harmonious manner, it still becomes a target when any sensitive issues occur.

1.4   Context and Arguments

This book is unified by a particular interest in understanding the challenges and issues posed by Chinese nationalists in practicing e-diplomacy on Weibo, because it indicates that the dominant assumption about social media ultimately being an ideal channel for two-way symmetrical communication might be problematic. This book sits in the background of understanding China's current wave of nationalism. The key feature of "love for the country" and "love of the Communist Party" of the current wave needs to be explained at this point.

Xi's "Chinese dream," for example, emphasizes wealth, national pride, and obedience to authority. Media and schools stress the idea of patriotism, with "love of country" considered conterminous with "love of the Communist Party." Ideas such as democracy, human rights, and modernization are mentioned as well, but generally with the appendage "with Chinese characteristics," to indicate that they have been modified to fit into Communist Party (China Daily Mail 2015).

One of the illustrations to this current wave of nationalism is the national flag snapshot event called "Let's take a photo with our national flag" in 2014, initiated by an overseas Chinese student in Australia; this event was endorsed and echoed by thousands of Chinese across the world via social media Weibo. This is a campaign asking Chinese Internet users to post snapshots of them and the national flag online has gone viral ahead of the 65th anniversary of the founding of the People's Republic of China on Wednesday. Pictures posted on Weibo, a Twitter-like microblogging platform, show Chinese posing all over the world. In one, a woman stands in front of a wall painted with a national flag. In another, several police officers present their smartphones bearing the national flag as the wallpaper. One girl took a selfie in front of a computer with the national flag as the background. Soldiers have also posted pictures of themselves standing guard at China's borders. In a short period, the campaign has become one of the hottest topics on Weibo, with more than 200 million comments. The campaign was initiated by Lei Xiying, a Chinese doctoral student studying in Australia. "Let's all pray for China, post a picture with the five-starred red flag and write blessings for our motherland," wrote Lei in a post. The student said he wanted people to express their patriotism.

Loving for its country is not unique, but one of the issues that poses a challenge to foreign embassies' is the ultranationalist sentiments towards "foreign hostile forces." In a propaganda video with slick production values that has gone viral on the Chinese Internet, Chinese nationalists warn viewers against what it says are US-led "foreign hostile forces" conspiring to foment a "colour revolution" similar to those in Ukraine, Georgia and the Arab Spring in mainland China (Wen 2016). This 5 min long video amassed more than 10 million views within 24 h. The video has had particular resonance in China given the way official party rhetoric has doubled down on its invective aimed at the prominent 4-day political show trial of lawyers and legal rights advocates, with the party-controlled judiciary portraying those on trial as having conspired with foreign agents to subvert the Chinese state, rather than seeking to advance rule of law in their country (Wen 2016).

1.5   NORMS VS REALITY

1.5.1   The Commonly Accounted Two-Way Communication Tool

Social media is one of the fastest growing tools of modern public diplomacy. Social media is believed to provide the right channel to reach youth populations, which is one of the major goals of current public diplomacy efforts. Researchers have started paying attention to social media and public relations/diplomacy in recent years, for example, in "New Media and Public Diplomacy in Network Society," Jordi Xifra analyzes the role of new media and social media in public relations, focuses on nation-building (Xifra 2012a, b). Xifra and Grau (2010) found that Twitter discourse related to public relations contributed more to practice than theory. Smith (2010) observed that communication power was shifting away from public relations practitioners to social media users whose organizational interests or roles may not be well defined, he suggests, this results "a social model of public relations in which traditional public relations responsibilities are distributed to social media users" (Smith 2010, p. 329). In his work, Smith emphasized that "scholars move beyond efforts to simply translate public relations models into online sphere... consider this an opportunity to consider new levels of risk, relationship, and interactivity" (p. 334).

From a public diplomacy perspective, the goal of utilizing ICTs, or e-diplomacy strategies, is the production, dissemination, and maintenance of knowledge that helps to further state interests (Harris 2013).

The advent of these technologies has fundamentally changed the ways state can both engage and inform foreign audiences:

> In the past a competent diplomat might have been able to reach hundreds and possibly thousands of individuals through external engagement. For a rare few, it might have been possible to occasionally reach hundreds of thousands or millions of people via newspapers, radio and television, but that required going through gatekeepers.
>
> Social media has changed this old dynamic. [The State Department] now effectively operates its own global media empire reaching more than eight million people directly through its 600 plus social media platforms. To provide a sense of the scale of this operation, this reach is as large as the paid subscriber base of the ten largest circulating daily newspapers in the USA, combined (although the impact and influence of the two platforms is likely quite different). This reach is still considerably smaller than Voice of America's estimated 187 million weekly audience, but [the State Department] has no editorial control over its content. After launching State's new Turkish Twitter feed Deputy Assistant Secretary of Public Affairs for Digital Strategy Victoria Esser put it this way: 'We are always seeking to expand the ways in which we can inform and engage... Social media offered us a way to do that in real time with much broader reach than we could ever hope for with traditional shoe leather public diplomacy. (Hanson 2012, p. 17).

1.5.2   Social Media's "Chinese Characteristics"

There is no doubt that scholars and journalists believe that social media like Weibo could be used as an effective platform for foreign public diplomacy practitioners to promote "two-way" communications. However, the use of social media has its "Chinese characteristics," which is "brushed with nationalistic sentiments."

The history of Chinese nationalism is of longstanding: some scholars argue that nationalism was transformed from Confucianism, which already existed in ancient China (Levenson 1964; Lin 1979; Schwartz 1964). Others argue that it originated in 1895 after the first Sino-Japan War and formed in the context of anti-foreignism (Wei and Liu 2001, p. 102; Zhao 2004). As I have argued that the nation-state and national identity are two fundamental elements of nationalism, I agree with the latter, because before 1895, the key elements of nation-state mentality and nationality were missing in China (Wei and Liu 2001, p. 102).

Prior to the war, the Chinese nation did not even have an official name or a real national flag, let alone the element of nation-state. Liang Qichao, one of the most influential Chinese scholar and journalist at that time wrote, "nothing makes me more ashamed than the fact that our nation has no name" (Liang 1989a, p. 3), and "we Chinese had no idea of the nation-state" (Liang 1959, p. 35). Sinologist and historian Immanuel C.Y. Hsu also noted, "doubtless, imperial China was not a nation-state" (Hsu 1960, p. 69). China did not wake up from its dream until the Sino-Japanese War when defeated by long-despised Japan and the loss of Hong Kong and other territories to Britain and other European powers. To quote Liang Qichao again, the first Sino-Japanese War, "awakened China from the great dream of four thousand years" (Liang 1989b, p. 113). After the Sino-Japanese War, Chinese people not only realized that China was not the Middle Kingdom of the world anymore, but also accepted the equality of the states in the world, as well as concepts such as the nation-state and national sovereignty (Wei and Liu 2001, pp. 102–103). As Murata Yujiro concluded, "the concept of the nation-state replete with sovereignty and territory took shape in modern China at the end of the nineteenth century after the defeat in the Sino-Japanese War" (Yujiro 1997, p. 113).

For Chinese intellectuals that time, the Sino-Japanese War left them with a new concept: a strong national identity was extremely important for constructing a strong Chinese nation-state (Wei and Liu 2001, p. 103). And this new concept became the intellectual and political basis for the formation of China's nationalism (ibid.). Therefore, as Zhao concludes,

> whereas European nationalism developed in an indigenous process driven by the combined force of mercantilism and liberalism, nationalist consciousness in China was triggered by external stimulus" (Zhao 2004, p. 50).

Hence, "external stimulus" was the derivation of Chinese nationalism, and the term Zhonghua minzu (Chinese people or nation) was connected tightly with the nationalistic warnings of the danger of national annihilation under external invasion (Dittmer and Kim 1993, p. 252).

Also, the suffering of defeats in a series of military confrontations with the West in the century of what Chinese called the "Century of Humiliation" (from mid-1800s) gave rise to Chinese nationalism (Zhao 2004, p. 50).

It is necessary to stop here, let me explain why it is called "Century of Humiliation" as an ethnic Chinese. In 1636, the Manchus renamed their kingdom Qing and took over China from the Han (Wang 1998, p. 11). The rulers of the Qing Dynasty viewed the Emperor as the Son of Heaven and the Chinese considered themselves as the center of the universe (Tyson 1995, p. 116). The Chinese name for China, Zhongguo, translated to "The Middle Kingdom" illustrates their feeling of being the center of the universe. The Qing Dynasty looked upon foreigners as barbarians, hence, did not want to open China for trade with other countries (Wang 1998). Although the rulers of Qing declared the only legal port, Guangzhou in Canton for foreign trade in 1757, the strict foreign trade policy that time caused strained relationships between China and other countries (Dillon 1998, p. 38).

The Qing Dynasty encountered many problems during the nineteenth century when China had lost both Opium Wars, and the country was in both economic and military decline. Due to the heavy loans and debts from the war, the Qing government had to not only increase taxes to pay for the cost of the war, but also increase foreign trade (Scott 2008, p. 11). The increasing foreign trade opened the gate of China, and accelerated the arrival of the century of China's "pushing around by outside powers," from 1842 to World War Two (ibid. p. 12). China had to sign a series of "unequal treaties" with Western countries and Japan, which weakened both the country's territory integrity and its sovereignty (Wang 1998). This century was its "bainian guochi" (Century of Humiliation). Therefore, these events determined that Chinese nationalism would contain a strong anti-foreign sentiment.

1.6   THEORETICAL FRAMEWORKS AND METHODS

This thesis opens up an interdisciplinary dialog and is situated between cultural studies and Internet studies. In terms of Internet studies, it is important to look to a theoretical reorientation based on not only empirical research but also the reality of the sociocultural context in China. To find out how effective is the use of Weibo to engage with Chinese citizens by foreign embassies in China, research on the use of Weibo and nationalism should focus on the implication of nationalistic sentiments expression on the assumed ideal platform for public diplomacy/public relations.

Therefore, this thesis discusses the employment of Chinese Weibo for foreign e-diplomacy practice around "nationalism," "global public relations theory" while viewing "global PR theory" as a framework for discussions in most chapters. Therefore, the next chapter of this thesis, Chap. 2, provides the theoretical foundation to the thesis by explicating and situating Grunig's global public relations theory—to make sense of China's case towards the practicing of public diplomacy via Weibo in China. Other concepts most frequently referred to in this thesis include "nationalism." Those concepts are all enabled in the conflict between two-way communications and the "foreign hostility" in each discussion, in order to understand why I propose the two-way systematic communication model is not practical in Weibo e-diplomacy, and to make sense of the many contradictory discourses in and about China's cyberspace.

The sources and methods in this thesis have been the combination between qualitative and quantitative research. Most of the chapters combine empirical research, textual analysis, discourse analysis, and contextual analysis in order to address the proposed research questions and research aims of this thesis. I apply these different approaches to evaluate three components which I consider essential to assessing the effectiveness of the use of Weibo by foreign embassies, namely "interactivity," "popularity," and "attitude." Quantitative research was also undertaken to examine the Weibo practice in China, specifically, the foreign embassies' use of Weibo in China. It includes both typological analysis and statistical analysis of Chinese Weibo practice.

1.7   SUMMARY OF THE THESIS

The thesis is composed of three parts. Part One (in this chapter and Chap. 2) is the introductory part of the book. In this chapter draws out the sketch of what the "problem" this thesis is dealing with, and clarifies the fundamental question this thesis examines: Is China's cyber-nationalism bringing any challenges to foreign embassies' practice of e-diplomacy in China? If it is, what sort of challenges is cyber-nationalism bringing to e-diplomacy? Chapter 2 sets up the background and provides the theoretical foundation of this thesis. Background briefing includes the social media landscape in China, nationalism waves in China, and Grunig's global PR theory.

Part Two (Chaps. 3, 4, and 5) deconstructs the "problem" by evaluating possible explanation to it. Chapter 3, "Scanning the foreign use of Weibo" introduces the practice of e-diplomacy on Weibo by foreign embassies in Beijing. The key aim of this chapter is to bring an overall picture of foreign use of Weibo and identify the top five embassies that uses Weibo frequently. It seeks to address three gaps in existing knowledge by empirical research. Firstly, at present, we simply do not know—in a systematic sense—what foreign embassies are doing on Weibo. We do not know which embassies have the most followers on Weibo, how often they Weibo, and what they are posting about.

Secondly, this chapter seeks to address the fact that we do not have a clear understanding of the benefit that foreign embassies are gaining from the Chinese online platform. It is not clear that what these benefits are due to their Weibo behavior.

Finally, this chapter seeks to address the deeper question: what the uptake of foreign embassy users of Chinese social media—and Chinese Weibo in particular—means for public diplomacy. Does Weibo offer better ways for public diplomacy workers to communicate with potential audience, or is it instead a fragmentary, dangerous, and disempowering distraction?

Chapter 4, "The Use of Chinese Social Media by Foreign Embassies: Interactivity VS Influence," focuses on measuring the interactivity of those foreign embassies' Weibo accounts. It was found that awareness does not imply positive influence. Defining public diplomacy (PD) as communication with foreign publics for the purpose of achieving a foreign policy objective, PD practitioners should be cognizant that information is different than influence (Wallin 2013). It was also found and echoed by other researchers that the number of followers does not necessarily equate a strong connection with an audience. An account might have a million followers say nothing, even though a post gets retweeted 1000 times per day, it doesn't indicate whether those followers are supporting or against the user's communication goals.

Chapter 5, "A close case study: Kunming terror attack & embassy's e-diplomacy via Weibo," aims to demonstrate empirically the challenges posed by Chinese cyber-nationalism in the practice of e-diplomacy on Weibo.

Part Three discusses the application of the use of Weibo by foreign embassies. Chapter 6, "Weibo as a public diplomacy tool," borrows the "three-dimension framework" from Bjola and Jiang (2015), discusses each dimension in relation to the empirical data in previous chapters.

Chapter 7, "Implications of foreign embassies' use of Weibo and global PR theory" dissects PR strategy and tactics into several dimensions and discuss them accordingly.

REFERENCES

Bjola, C. & Jiang, L. (2015). Social media and public diplomacy. In Bjola & Holmes (Eds.), *Digital diplomacy: Theory and practice* (pp. 71–87). Routledge, London.

China Daily Mail. (2015, May 4). *What it means to be Chinese—nationalism and identity in Xi's China.* Retrieved August 23, 2016, from https://chinadailymail.com/2015/05/04/what-it-means-to-be-chinese-nationalism-and-identity-in-xis-china/.

ChinaLabs. (2013a, October). *The report on the effectiveness of using Internet by foreign embassies in China, Chinalabs.* Retrieved August 22, 2015, from http://www.huanqiu.com/attach/country/the_influence_of_websites_of_foreign_embassies_in_china_pdf.pdf.

ChinaLabs. (2013b, October). *Research report on the impact of foreign embassies' online engagement with Chinese citizens.* Retrieved August 23, 2016, from http://www.huanqiu.com/attach/country/the_influence_of_websites.

CNNIC. (2013). The 31st statistical report on internet development. *CNNIC.* Retrieved February 28, 2014, from http://www1.cnnic.cn/AU/SocialR/SocialNews/201301/t20130121_38607.htm.

CNNIC. (2015). Statistical report on internet development in China, China internet network information centre, January 2015. Retrieved June 7, 2017, from https://cnnic.com.cn/IDR/ReportDownloads/201507/P020150720 486421654597.pdf.

Comor, D. & Bean, H.(2012). America's 'engagement' delusion: Critiquing a public diplomacy consensus. *International Communication Gazette, 74*(3), 203–220.

Cull, N. J. (2010). Public diplomacy: Seven lessons for its future from its past. *Place branding and public diplomacy, 6*(1), 11–17.

Cull, N. J. (2013). The long road to public diplomacy 2.0: The internet in US public diplomacy. *International Studies Review, 15*(1), 123–139.

Dillon, M. (Ed.). (1998). *China: A historical and cultural dictionary.* London: Routledge.

Dittmer, L., & Kim, S. (1993). Whither China's quest for national identity? In *China's quest for national identity.* Ithaca, NY: Cornell University Press.

Gao, Z. (2013). China's sina dominates weibo by faking followers. *The Epoch Times.* Retrieved February 28, 2014, from http://www.theepochtimes.com/ n2/china-news/chinas-sina-dominates-Weibo-by-faking-followers-351661. html.

Hanson, F. (2012). *Revolution@ state: The spread of ediplomacy.* Sydney: Lowy Institute for International Policy.

Harris, B. (2013). *Diplomacy 2.0: The future of social media in nation branding.* Retrieved September 20, 2015, from http://surface.syr.edu/cgi/viewcontent.cgi?article=1032&context=exchange.

Hoffman, D. (2002). Beyond public diplomacy. *Foreign Affairs, 81* 83–95.

Hsu, I. (1960). *China's entrance into the family of nations: The diplomatic phase, 1858–1880.* Cambridge, MA: Harvard University Press.

J.M. (2013). Social stability: The case for a heavy hand, *The Economist,* 14 Decmber 2013. Retrieved on June 8, 2017 from http://www.economist. com/blogs/analects/2013/12/social-stability.

Jiang, Y. (2012). *Cyber-nationalism in China: Challenging western portrayal of Chinese censorship.* Adelaide: University of Adelaide Press.

Levenson, J. L. (1964). *Modern China and its confucian past: The problem of intellectual continuity.* New York: Anchor Books.

Liang, Q. (1959). *Xinmin shuo (on new citizenship).* Taipei: Zhonghua Shuju.

Liang, Q (1989a). 'Zhongguoshi xulun' (A narrative analysis of Chinese history). In *Yinbingshi heji* (Vol. 1, p. 3). Beijing: Zhongguo Shuju.

Liang, Q. (1989b). 'Zhongguo liguo zhi dafangzhen' (The fundamental policies for China's being a nation-state). In *Yinbingshi heji* (Vol. 4, pp. 39–78). Beijing: Zhongguo Shuju.

Lin, Y. (1979). *The crisis of chinese consciousness.* Madison: The University of Wisconsin Press.

Mor, Ben D. (2012). Credibility talk in public diplomacy. *Review of International Studies, 38*(2), 393–422.

Parliament of Australia. (2012). Chapter 4 E-diplomacy. http://www.aph.gov. au/Parliamentary_Business/Committees/Joint/Completed_Inquiries/jfadt/ Overseas%20Representation/report/chapter4.

Schwartz, B. (1964). *In search of wealth and power.* New York: Harper Torchbook.

Scott, D. (2008). *China and the international system, 1840–1949:power, presence, and perceptions in a century of humiliation.* New York: SUNY Press.

Sina Weibo. (2015, December). *Weibo users development report*. Retrieved September 20, 2016, from http://data.weibo.com/report/reportDetail?id=297.

Smith, B. G. (2010). Socially distributing public relations: Twitter, Haiti, and interactivity in social media. *Public Relations Review, 36*(4), 329–335.

Tyson, A. (1995). *Chinese awakenings: Life stories from the unofficial China*. Boulder, CO: Westview Press.

Wallin, M. (2013, February). The challenges of the Internet and social media in public diplomacy, *American Security Project*. Accessed 12 January, 2016, from https://americansecurityproject.org/ASP%20Reports/Ref%200112%20-%20Challenges%20of%20the%20Internet%20and%20Social%20Media%20in%20PD.pdf.

Wang, K. W. (Ed.). (1998). *Modern China: An encyclopedia of history, culture, and nationalism*. New York: Garland Publishing.

Wei, C. X. G., & Liu, X. Y. (2001). *Chinese nationalism in perspective: Historical and recent cases*. Lanham, MD: Greenwood Publishing Group.

Wen, P. (2016, August 4). The Australian connection behind China's ultra-nationalist viral video. *Sydney Morning Herald*. http://www.smh.com.au/world/the-australian-connection-behind-chinas-ultranationalist-viral-video-20160803-gqkiki.html.

Xifra, J., & Grau, F. (2010). Nanoblogging in PR: The discourse on public relations in Twitter. *Public Relations Review, 36*(2), 171–174.

Xifra. (2012a). New media and public diplomacy in network society: Applying manuel castells' sociology to public relations. In Duhe (Ed.), *New media and public relations*. New York: Peter Lang.

Xifra, J. (2012b). New media and public diplomacy in network society-applying Manuel Castells' sociology to public society. In Duhe (Ed.), *New media and public relations* (2nd ed.). New York: Peter Lang.

Yujiro, M. (1997). Dynasty, state, and society: The case of modern China. In J. A. Fogel & P. G. Zarrow (Eds.), *Imagining the people: Chinese intellectual and the concept of citizenship* (pp. 1890–1929). Armonk, NY: M.E. Sharpe.

Zhao, S. S. (2004). *A nation-state by construction: Dynamics of modern Chinese nationalism*. Stanford, CA: Stanford University Press.

CHAPTER 2

Social Media Context in China and Global PR Theory

Abstract This chapter sets up the background and provides the theoretical foundation of this book. Background briefing includes the social media landscape in China, nationalism waves in China, and Grunig's global PR theory.

Keywords Social media · Nationalism · Global PR theory

2.1 INTRODUCTION

This chapter sets up the background of China's fast-growing social media landscape and provides the theoretical foundation to the thesis. Background briefing includes the demographics of China's social media users, Weibo use and control in China, and the cyber-nationalism in current China. In contrast with Chinese Weibo users' "unhappy" feeling about foreign embassies' "double-standard" in not calling the Kunming terror attack "terrorism", this chapter highlights the majority of Chinese Weibo users are content with the social media in China.

China's ongoing Internet revolution, which has had enthusiastic support from the government, is seen as the driving force of China's economic takeoff in the new millennium (Tai 2006, p. 120). But, while it is clear that China has adopted information and communication technologies as a cornerstone of its economic development, it has at the same time attempted to minimize the consequences they consider to be

© The Author(s) 2017
Y. Jiang, *Social Media and e-Diplomacy in China*,
DOI 10.1057/978-1-137-59358-0_2

undesirable, such as unsettling the one-party political framework and destroying their political control over society (Deibert 2002, p. 144; Xiao 2005). Internet control in mainland China is not only carried out under a wide variety of laws and administrative regulations, but also via social norms and through the market (Tsui 2001). These seemingly contradictory swings between economic liberalization and political control have characterized China's relationship with the outside world since 1994 (Chan 1994, p. 70), but with the continuous development of the Internet in China, with the grow up of China's Generation Y who are the mainstream Internet users in China, the contradiction between economic liberalization and political control seems to become more and more accepted by this particular generation. Chinese cyberspace has not only demonstrated the harmonious compatibility of "economic liberalization" and "political control," but also the harmonious compatibility of early stage political liberalization and the support of the existing political framework (Jiang 2012).

This chapter, therefore, sets up an overall picture of the Internet in China with a focus on such, what I called above, the "harmonious compatibilities." It aims to achieve three goals: to provide the brief background of social media in China for audience who don't possess strong knowledge of the cyberspace in China; to unveil the interesting compatibility of the extreme "apolitical" ideology that Generation Y holds and their extreme "political" passion in particular circumstances; and, most importantly, to look at how the compatibilities are challenging the practice of public diplomacy by introducing Grunig's global PR theory into the book for examination and for further discussion in the following chapters in the thesis. Therefore, this chapter not only provides information about the development, the demographics, the uses, and the control of social media, together with the dominant online consumer culture in China, but also provides the theoretical foundation to this chapter and the whole thesis by explicating the classic Grunig's four models of PR in a social media age. In this chapter, the enabling of Grunig's PR theories initiates understanding of Foreign Embassies' approach in practicing public diplomacy via social media platforms on the one hand, and the challenging variables they might face on the other. It suggests that social media platforms provide an unprecedent channel for public diplomacy practioners to face the targeting audience's nationalistic sentiments directly; therefore, it generates unprecedent issues that global PR practitioners need to solve. This book provides systemic empirical data to critically examine Grunig's global PR theories, and questions the assumed effective "two-way communication," which is one of the very rare available works in academia.

2.2   SOCIAL MEDIA IN CHINA AND WEIBO

The social media landscape in China is very different from the rest of the world. While Facebook, Twitter are regarded as the top two social media platforms in the world, neither of these two are available in China due to the country's Internet regulations. Instead, the three most popular social media in China are: Sina Weibo, Wechat, and Tencent Weibo. They will be introduced respectively in the following paragraphs.

As introduced in the opening section, Weibo is a Chinese microblogging (Weibo) website, in use by well over 30% of the world's Internet users, with a similar market penetration that Twitter has established in the USA. Although the most recent CNNIC (China Internet Network Information Center) report in December 2012 announced that there are 309 million Weibo users in China (CNNIC 2013), the announced numbers of Weibo users provided by each Weibo service providers are much higher than the figure this official report disclosed. This is probably due to the competition between each Weibo service providers, but scholars and journalists in China often use the estimation of more than 400 million, which is somewhere between CNNIC's official report and commercial Weibo service providers statistics.

It is important to note that, when Chinese people say "Weibo," it is commonly referred to Sina Weibo. However, Sina Weibo is just one of the various Weibo service competitors. Sina Weibo claims it has around 500 million registered accounts as of December 2012. Others include Tencent (the owner of QQ.com) which also alleged having a microblog site with 400 million registered accounts; and Sohu Weibo with over 100 million registered accounts. Therefore, it is more accurate to say "Tencent Weibo (Tenxun Weibo)" and "Sohu Weibo (Souhu Weibo)" to differentiate from "Sina Weibo (Xinlang Weibo)."

Due to its success of overseas users' penetration, Sina Weibo is still the most well-known Weibo service; therefore, the term Weibo used in this article refers to Sina Weibo.

Weibo, similar to Twitter, is more "conversational" than many other social media platforms. Weibo users can use 140 characters to share what's happening with others. The core element of Weibo is based on the model of human relations (Porter 2009). One doesn't need to become friends with others to be able to read each other's posts. One might follow 10,000 users while only 50 users follow oneself; one might only follow 5 users but having 10,000 users following one's own account.

China has Renren net equivalent to Facebook in the West; neither of them allows "conversation" between non-friends. So if Renren and Facebook are viewed as a lounge room in someone's house, Weibo and Twitter would be a bar or street plaza, because anyone who is interested in the topic can join the conversation despite whether you follow each other (Raymond 1999; Grant and Moon 2010). Therefore, Weibo and Twitter are closer to a public space, and have unique advantages of becoming effective communication tools for reputation management and community engagement. According to the 2010 statistical results published on WebBizideas.com, 26% of American corporations would pay for business functionality on Twitter (Hwang 2012). Celebrities in the world have also embraced this social media to gather more "followers" (Faina 2012; Marwick and Boyd 2012).

Weibo, like Twitter, restricts posts to a maximum of 140 characters. However, it is over simplistic to define Weibo as "Chinese versions of Twitter." Both Sina Weibo and Tencent Weibo are providing more complex and advanced services than Twitter, for example, allowing users to add comments when retweet, whereas Twitter doesn't allow this function. Due to the blockage of Twitter and Facebook in China, the social media landscape in China is dominated by domestic brands rather than these international big names. Chinese domestic companies such as Sina and Tencent are intent on developing more complex hybrids that build on their respective advantages as multifaceted web portals (Dashan 2012). Thus, it would be more accurate to say that Weibo refers to Chinese microblogs that are hybrids of both Twitter and Facebook (Dashan 2012).

2.3   Internet Censorship in China and Censorship on Weibo

China is not only famous for the Great Wall, but also the Great Firewall. According to the ONI, China has one of the largest and most sophisticated filtering systems. This section will provide an overall picture of the various representations of Internet censorship in China, then moving on to the explanation of how censorship works on Weibo.

2.3.1   Defensive and Offensive Censorship

Internet censorship mechanisms in China have demonstrated both defensive and offensive characteristics. It involves "removal" and "replacement" that prevents information from reaching the public, as well as "displacement" and "dispersal" that disseminate a particular version to the mass public so that other perspectives are drowned out. While the defensive censorship filters the information unwanted by the government, the offensive censorship is filtering in a converse way: it filters through only the wanted contents. Defensive censorship is predominantly used in Chinese cyberspace; the widely circulated list of banned words in Chinese cyberspace tells us there are more than 1000 taboo terms (Xiao 2004; Pan 2006; Weiquan Wang 2008). On the other hand, offensive censorship often acts upon unpredictable significant negative incidents when information cannot be simply blocked. Therefore, offensive censorship works as a complementary to the defensive censorship. For example, in both the cases of the SARS disease in 2003 and the poisoned milk powder incident in 2008, instead of completely banning the information from reaching the mass, government officials made positive announcements to the public at the early stage of the incidents (BBC 2008).

2.3.2   Structural and Deliberate Censorship

While deliberate censorship is to censor materials that are against government's censorship laws and regulations, structural censorship functions through the market. Deliberate censorship plays an important role in the filtering of China's Internet. As the brief overview of Internet censorship around the world indicates, in the West, while Internet regulations that control the transmission of child pornography or specify hatred speech do exist in most countries, they do not filter Internet contents on a state level. In comparison, China's legal regulation of the Internet is extraordinarily complicated.

On the other hand, Internet censorship in China also takes effects through the market. This is particular the case of the foreign enterprises that do business in China. From Fortune 500 companies in China to Google, Yahoo!, Skype, and Websense, foreign companies in China are helping Chinese government to censor Chinese users while they are pursuing their profits through the market. Foreign companies deny they have signed any contract with Chinese central government; they state that it is the users in China who choose to block which is beyond their control (Hu 2002). For example, when Microsoft responded to Human rights group Amnesty International, a human rights organization which is working on the improvement of freedom of expression in the world, it is said that it is "focused on delivering the best technology to people throughout the world. However, Microsoft cannot control the way it may ultimately be used" (Hu 2002).

2.3.3   Direct and Subtle Censorship

Direct censorship is a top-down operation, carried out by the government and its agents with the exercise of sovereign power. Subtle censorship, on the other hand, is structural and largely involves the "technologies of the self." According to Amnesty International, China has continuously arrested Internet activists since 1998 for the manifest reason of breaching Internet laws. Chinese police have been arresting suspects in the name of cracking down Internet pornography every year, followers on Sina Weibo and was seen by many as an online crusader for justice (Ford 2013). But while direct censorship such as the punitive Internet laws in China that cause imprisonments of Internet activisms still exists, it is noticed that subtle censorship is more implemented by Chinese government nowadays. As MacKinnon observed in 2009, "the Chinese government's Internet strategy is placing increasing emphasis on corporate self-censorship, spin and manipulation to supplement 'firewall' blocking" (MacKinnon 2009).

2.3.4   Weibo Censorship

The boom of social media in China was considered to pose a challenge to the existing censorship mechanisms in China, because the daily turn out of posts is huge. But what has been confirmed in practices is that Sina Weibo uses various methods to censor user-generated contents, from not allowing users to upload undesired entries, to "privatizing" a successfully uploaded entry from being viewed by others, to deleting an entry several hours or days after the manual after-post censoring process. McNaughton (2012) summarized how the process works:

- Sina Weibo's computer system scans each microblog before it is published
- a "fraction" of these posts are marked as sensitive and read by a censor
- the censor then decides whether to delete it
- posts with "must kill" words (references to banned groups, etc.) are blocked and manually deleted
- censors update lists of sensitive words as bloggers create new expressions to avoid censorship

The new seven bottom lines (七条底线) issued by the government in 2013 have become online codes of conduct covering seven areas, namely:

1. Laws and regulations;
2. Socialist system;
3. State interests;
4. Citizen's legal rights;
5. Social and public order;
6. Morality;
7. Truth of information.

Chinese officials recently have ordered Chinese media outlets to "strengthen information management," "crack down on false rumors". These orders and above-mentioned "new seven bottom lines" are broad and vague. There's a blanket ban on anything that would harm state security and social stability. While the specific codes are yet to be fleshed out, they indicate the seven areas in which the authorities intend to keep a strict watch over online information. Based on the author's empirical analysis, the presentation of censorship on Weibo is categorised into following scenarios:

1. Before posting keywords filtering—not allowing users to upload undesired entries (Fig. 2.1)
   Translation by author: sorry, this post is a violation of ⟨ Sina Weibo Community Management Rules ⟩ or other relevant policy and law.
2. After posting (scenario 1) blocking a successfully uploaded entry from being viewed by others (Fig. 2.2)
   Translation by author: sorry, the post you made on 8 May 2012 at 18:33:01 titled "Communist Party is a good party" has been

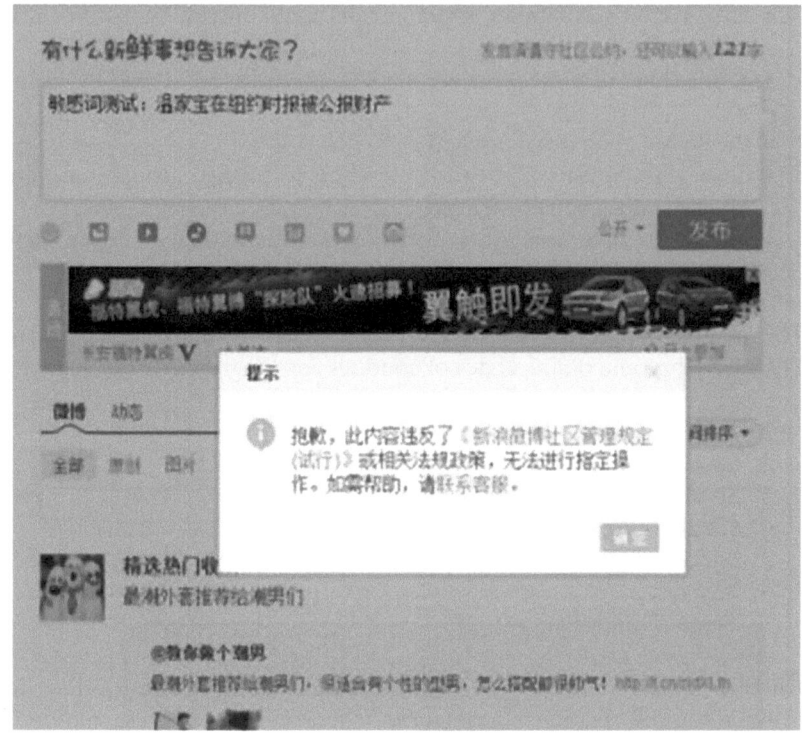

Fig. 2.1 Weibo censorship representation. *Source* screenshot from author's Weibo page

classified by system manager. This post is not suitable for publishing. If you need help, please contact customer service.

3. After posting (scenario 2) deleting an entry several hours or days after the manual after-post censoring process (Fig. 2.3).

Translation by author: sorry, this post has been deleted.

Although current Weibo censorship is mainly targeting on texts, this doesn't mean images published on Weibo are ignored. ProPublica has been tracking 100 Weibo accounts, noting which posts had images and returning to see if these images had been deleted. Out of 80,000 posts so far, at least 4200—more than 5%—got deleted by censors. Political

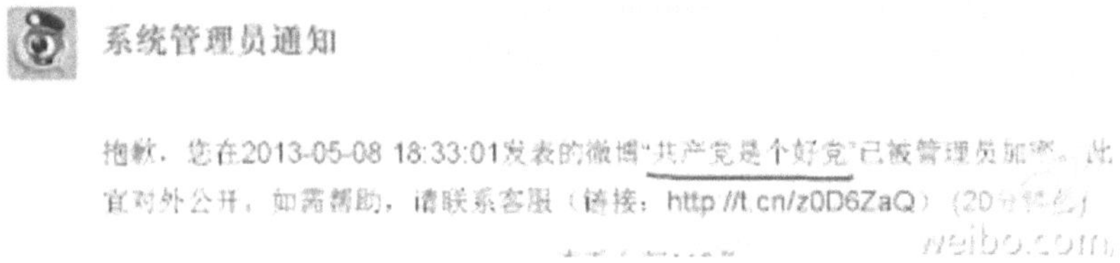

系统管理员通知

抱歉，您在2013-05-08 18:33:01发表的微博"共产党是个好党"已被管理员加密。此官对外公开，如需帮助，请联系客服（链接：http://t.cn/zOD6ZaQ）(20)
weibo.com

Fig. 2.2 Weibo censorship representation. *Source* screenshot from author's Weibo page

川美陈俊 ★：//@叶海燕先生 法律已死。这行为艺术的表达真直白。//这算不算报应？施酷刑的吴承奋40多岁得了脑癌；指令要做有罪判决原福州政~注委宋立诚书记判刑13年；专案组长福清市公安局林孜局长涉黑于2003年判刑16年；//@那个三疯子 开始怀疑恶有恶报是否真的存在 为什么一群流氓霸占着法律却能为所欲为？

抱歉，此微博已被作者删除。查看帮助：http://t.cn/zWSudZc

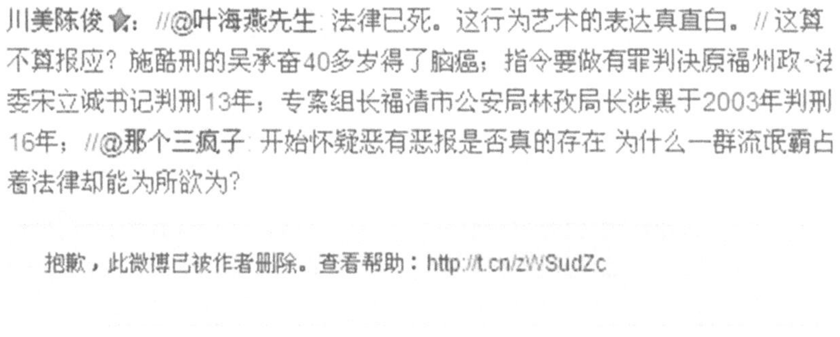

Fig. 2.3 Weibo censorship representation. *Source* screenshot from author's Weibo page

speeches—anything that portrays the government or the Communist Party in a negative light—formed the largest category of censored images. These are followed by images with huge chunks of text that elaborate on anti-government ideas, such as politically charged essays, petitions to release activists, and interview transcripts.

2.4   Effecting Grunig's Global PR Theory

2.4.1   The "Four Models"

The most-cited piece of public relations work to date is the 1984 textbook *Managing Public Relations* by James E. Grunig and Todd Hunt (Pasadeos et al. 2010). Grunig and Hunt established four models of public relations, which include press agentry/publicity, public information, two-way asymmetric, and two-way symmetric communication. Grunig and Hunt suggest that the two-way symmetrical model, which advocates mutual understanding and dialog, is the one to aspire towards in terms of best practice and ethics within public relations. The "4 Models" describe distinct approaches to public relations in the context of a 130-year timeline that shows how public relations has evolved.

James Grunig (2009) has recently applied his four models of public relations to social media. James Grunig (2009) argues in favor of two-way communication and highlights the significance social media can have on this dialogic communication. He states that social media used to its full potential can provide public relations with a more two-way and interactive, global, strategic, and socially responsible approach. Furthermore, Grunig comments in the same text on the importance of different publics. He argues that the relationship with an organization's immediate publics is what matters and that organizations do not need relationships with other publics. This is a rather controversial point, especially in regard to social media where most content is open for everyone (Phillips and Young 2009). Critics of this view, such as Jensen (2001), argue that audiences that might not be seen as key publics could still be important since they might engage in discussions that consequently will affect the organization's key publics and their interests. Ihlen agrees with this point of view and argues "people, who do not seem like stakeholders at the present, might choose to take interest in a company at a later stage" (Ihlen 2008, p. 142). Some might argue that there is a fear of losing control over messages when they are spread online but others claim that the advantages of broadening conversations are more important (Kanter and Fine 2010).

2.4.2   Excellence Theory

The excellence theory of public relations is a fundamental and defining statement about what effective public relations is. The excellence theory is the result of a 15-year comprehensive study to determine what are the characteristics of excellent communications and of the companies that do excellent public relations. The excellence theory is a general theory of public relations "specifies how public relations makes organizations more effective, how it is organized and managed when it contributes most to organizational effectiveness, the conditions in organizations and their environments that make organizations more effective, and how the monetary value of public relations can be determined." The excellence theory resulted from a study about the best practice in public relations, which was headed by James E. Grunig and funded by the Foundation of the International Association of Business Communicators (IABC) in 1985. Constructed upon a number of middle-range theories, and tested with surveys and interviews of professionals and CEOs in the USA, the UK, and Canada, the Excellence theory provides a "theoretical and empirical benchmark" for public relations units.

The excellence theory explained that the value of public relations lies in organization–public relations. Good relationship with its strategic publics is helpful for an organization to develop and achieve goals desired by both the organization and its publics, reduce costs of negative publicity, and increase revenue by providing products and services needed by stakeholders. To maximize value of public relations, public relations must identify strategic publics and build long-term relationships with them through symmetrical communication programs. The excellence study identified characteristics of effective public relations in four major categories:

1. Empowerment of public relations function: effective organization must empower public relations as a critical management function.
2. Communicator roles: let public relations executives play managerial role as well as administrative role.
3. Organization of communication function: public relations should be an integrated communication function and separate from instead of being sublimated to marketing or other management functions.
4. Public relations models: effect organization should base its internal and external communication and relationship building on two-way symmetrical model.

2.4.3   The Global PR Theory

During the last decade, scholars have replicated excellence study around the world. Results from these studies extended the Excellence theory into a global public relations theory, which provides generic principles that are understood in the same way around the world and can be operated effectively in most nations. The global public relations theory also suggests that practice in different countries should be different based on culture, political system, economic system, media system, level of economic development, and extent and nature of activism in a certain country.

2.4.4   Critiques

Many scholars have questioned the possibility of the two-way symmetrical model in real-life context. Van der Meiden observed that the two-way symmetrical model is unrealistic since it suggests that organizations should value the interests of their publics more than those of the organization. Murphy 1991 proposed that the concept of symmetrical communication works along a continuum from pure conflict to pure cooperation, which is based on mixed motives. Leichty 1997 argued that completely collaborative public relations is not feasible in some situations, and pointed out that public relations practitioners' lack of power within an organization further increases the limitation of collaboration.

2.5   Understanding China's Nationalism

On 20th March 2009, a new book called *Unhappy China* was released in China. This book is a follow-up to the intensely nationalistic 1996 bestseller, *China Can Say No*. The authors of this new book remind us of something which surprised the authors and China's old generations: China's young generation's prompt reaction to Western media representations of China's actions during the torch relay. What this "surprising" reaction also indicates is a crucial factor in examining the political implications of China's Internet: any "political change" in contemporary China will be unlikely to change its existing political framework. This chapter is devoted to discussion of this indicative trend.

The quotation above signals the ultimate differences between China's Generation Y's nationalism and the previous generational waves. What has shocked domestic Chinese is the anti-Western actions of this generation, often derided as a generation "addicted to the Internet," "addicted to capitalism," or "apathetic around politics." A dislike of Western ideology has been a consistent theme of Chinese nationalism after 1989 (Gries 2004; Zheng 1999); however, this new wave of Chinese nationalism indicates a new anti-West model that is different from its predecessors: consumption of Western culture yet resentment of Western political ideology. While more and more young Chinese are consuming Western products such as Starbucks's coffee, or wearing Adidas shoes, getting Western degrees, and even becoming permanent residents of Western countries, the love for their motherland China is also getting stronger and stronger. In 2014, a Chinese overseas student in Australia initiated an online event called "Take a photography with our national flag" on Weibo, calls for all overseas Chinese in the world to take a photo with themselves and the Chinese national flag and post them on Weibo to demonstrate their "love for the motherland—China" (see Fig. 2.1). This online event was echoed by millions Chinese globally. Loving one's motherland is not only a Chinese phenomenon, but the point I make here is that this "love for the motherland" has been largely in the presentation of supporting the central government and dislike any critical coverage of China on the global stage, despite the corruptions of local government which have been exposed in a lot of cases.

The history of Chinese nationalism is of longstanding: some scholars argue that nationalism was transformed from Confucianism, which already existed in ancient China (Levenson 1964; Lin 1979; Schwartz 1964). Others argue that it originated in 1895 after the first Sino-Japan War and formed in the context of anti-foreignism (Wei and Liu 2001, p. 102; Zhao 2004). As I have argued that the nation-state and national identity are two fundamental elements of nationalism, I agree with the latter, because before 1895, the key elements of nation-state mentality and nationality were missing in China (Wei and Liu 2001, p. 102).

Prior to the war, the Chinese nation did not even have an official name or a real national flag, let alone the element of nation-state. Liang Qichao, one of the most influential Chinese scholar and journalist at that time wrote, "nothing makes me more ashamed than the fact that our nation has no name" (Liang 1989a, p. 3), and "we Chinese had no idea of the nation-state" (Liang 1959, p. 35). Sinologist and historian Immanuel C.Y. Hsu also noted, "doubtless, imperial China was not a nation-state" (Hsu 1960, p. 69). China did not wake up from its dream until the Sino-Japanese War when defeated by long-despised Japan and the loss of Hong Kong and other territories to Britain and other European powers. To quote Liang Qichao again, the first Sino-Japanese War, "awakened China from the great dream of four thousand years" (Liang 1989b, p. 113). After the Sino-Japanese War, Chinese people not only realized that China was not the Middle Kingdom of the world anymore, but also accepted the equality of the states in the world, as well as concepts such as the nation-state and national sovereignty (Wei and Liu 2001, pp. 102–103). As Murata Yujiro concluded, "the concept of the nation-state replete with sovereignty and territory took shape in modern China at the end of the nineteenth century after the defeat in the Sino-Japanese War" (Yujiro 1997, p. 113).

For Chinese intellectuals that time, the Sino-Japanese War left them with a new concept: a strong national identity was extremely important for constructing a strong Chinese nation-state (Wei and Liu 2001, p. 103). And this new concept became the intellectual and political basis for the formation of China's nationalism (ibid.). Therefore, as Zhao concludes,

> whereas European nationalism developed in an indigenous process driven by the combined force of mercantilism and liberalism, nationalist consciousness in China was triggered by external stimulus" (Zhao 2004, p. 50).

Hence, "external stimulus" was the derivation of Chinese nationalism, and the term Zhonghua minzu (Chinese people or nation) was connected tightly with the nationalistic warnings of the danger of national annihilation under external invasion (Dittmer and Kim 1993, p. 252).

Also, the suffering of defeats in a series of military confrontations with the West in the century of what Chinese called the "Century of Humiliation" (from mid-1800s) gave rise to Chinese nationalism (Zhao 2004, p. 50).

It is necessary to stop here, let me explain why it is called "Century of Humiliation" as an ethnic Chinese. In 1636, the Manchus renamed their kingdom Qing and took over China from the Han (Wang 1998, p. 11). The rulers of the Qing Dynasty viewed the Emperor as the Son of Heaven and the Chinese considered themselves as the center of the universe (Tyson 1995, p. 116). The Chinese name for China, Zhongguo, translated to "The Middle Kingdom" illustrates their feeling of being the center of the universe. The Qing Dynasty looked upon foreigners as barbarians, hence, did not want to open China for trade with other countries (Wang 1998). Although the rulers of Qing declared the only legal port, Guangzhou in Canton for foreign trade in 1757, the strict foreign trade policy that time caused strained relationships between China and other countries (Dillon 1998, p. 38).

The Qing Dynasty encountered many problems during the nineteenth century when China had lost both Opium Wars, and the country was in both economic and military decline. Due to the heavy loans and debts from the war, the Qing government had to not only increase taxes to pay for the cost of the war, but also increase foreign trade. The increasing foreign trade opened the gate of China, and accelerated the arrival of the century of China's "pushing around by outside powers," from 1842 to World War Two (ibid., p. 12). China had to sign a series of "unequal treaties" with Western countries and Japan, which weakened both the country's territory integrity and its sovereignty (Wang 1998). This century was its "bainian guochi" (Century of Humiliation).

Therefore, these events determined that Chinese nationalism would contain a strong anti-foreign sentiment. But how should the rise of China's Generation Y's resentment to the West today be understood? Is it a continuation of the old anti-foreign sentiment or does it represent something new? This is perhaps the central issue in understanding China's nationalism today, so let me carry this question forward for investigation.

It is not necessary to go through the whole history of Chinese nationalism in a study like this, the first major changing point of Chinese nationalistic sentiment was when the CCP took power in 1949. Therefore, I will trace back Chinese nationalism to 1949 when the People's Republic of China was founded by the CCP. But even analyzing Chinese nationalism from 1949 to 2008 is difficult in a short overview like this, not only because the definition of nationalism itself is ambiguous but also because, as Wang Gungwu points out, the study of Chinese nationalism is a many-layered and multifaceted phenomenon (Wang 1996, cited in Zheng 1999, p. x). Thus, it is difficult to highlight all aspects of Chinese nationalism in a single study. To make it manageable and to make it more relevant to this particular research, I will divide Chinese nationalism from 1949 to 2008 into four phases, the Mao era; 1976–1989 (after Mao's death before the Tiananmen Square incident); 1989–2001 (after the Tiananmen Square incident before China was elected to host the 2008 Olympics); and 2001–2008 (the preparation and the host of Beijing Olympics). I will focus on the attitudes toward Western ideologies in each period, and the exercises of governmental power in forming these attitudes.

In 1949, the Chinese Communist Party (CCP) founded the new China on the basis of anti-Japanese sentiments. The CCP has built its legitimacy on its nationalist credentials ever since. Hence, Chinese nationalism was expressed in a "victor narrative" of heroic Chinese victories over Western and Japanese imperialism at that time (ibid., p. 106).

The nationalistic sentiments continued its anti-imperialist narrative, but more importantly, contained the strong worship for the leader, Chairman Mao Tse-tung, due to Mao's mythic heroic image-building strategy (Chang 2003). It was exercised from the top based on the worship for the top leader, Mao. Mao was seen as a true nationalist and is widely credited with restoring China's dignity (Zheng 1999; Kluver 1996). As Kluver describes,

> Mao stood atop the Gate of Heavenly Peace in 1949 and proclaimed that 'The Chinese people have stood up', thus visually illustrating his point while further fusing his image with the national identity of the Chinese people (Kluver 1996, p. 28).

The CCP came into power on the basis of anti-Western and Japanese imperialism in 1949, it then proceeded to "chisel out a national identity by introducing the Soviet Union as the dreamland" after the new Chinese nation was built (Wei et al. 2002, p. 83). The CCP followed its Soviet Union brother's revolutionary journey, adopted the Marxist–Leninist doctrine of nationalism which political behavior can be reduced to economic interests (Zheng 1999, p. 69). Therefore, nationalism was regarded as either a "disguised economic interest" or in Marxist term as "false consciousness" that misled people and stopped them from pursuing their "true" class interests (ibid.). The whole country was enthusiastic for close connections with the Soviet Union: invitations to Soviet specialists became national policy, and every area of administration was open and ready for Soviet instruction (Wei et al. 2002, pp. 83–86). But Mao soon found this "apprenticeship" was in serious conflict with the goal of the Chinese nationalists; that is, to build a strong and independent nation-state (ibid., pp. 90–94). This conflicting interest ended up China's honeymoon with the Soviet Union in 1960 (Zheng 1999, p. 69). The concept of nationalism was then replaced with "patriotism," and to build a strong Chinese nation as a whole so that it becomes the identity of all Chinese was strengthened by the CCP (Zheng 1999, p. 70). Mao's ideology of "patriotism" can be interpreted as anti-imperialism, anti-feudalism, anti-Confucianism, and anti-capitalism (Zhang 2001, p. 264). The mythic image of Mao was then used to help stabilize the new government and legitimize the policies of the new government.

Scholars have described Mao as the greatest hero of the Chinese national epic (Chang and Halliday 2005; Kluver 1996; Teiwes 1996).

The Cultural Revolution which brought the nation chaos illustrates the rhetorical power of Mao's mythic image best. Jung Chang describes the mysterious cult of Mao in her memoirs of growing up during the Culture Revolution:

> Mao made himself more godlike by shrouding himself in mystery. He always appeared remote, beyond human approach... Mao, the emperor, fitted one of the patterns of Chinese history: the leader of a nationwide peasant uprising who swept away a rotten dynasty and became a wise new emperor exercising absolute authority. And, in a sense, Mao could be said to have earned his god-emperor status. He was responsible for ending the civil war and bringing peace and stability... It was under Mao that China became a power to be reckoned with in the world, and many Chinese stopped feeling ashamed and humiliated at being Chinese (Chang 2003, p. 137).

After the death of Mao in 1976, Deng Xiaoping started a modernization program aimed at making China stronger and richer. From 1976 to 1989, Chinese nationalism was switched to a phase of pro-Western ideologies. During this phase and before the crash down on the 1989 Tiananmen movement, the exercise of "pastoral power" that is "tied up with its notion of the living individual and his/her needs" took place (Dean 1991, p. 81). With the implementation of the reform and opening policy in the 1980s, the living standards of Chinese people improved significantly due to the rapid economic growth (Zheng 1999, p. 50). Between 1981 and 1991, the ratio of household color television set increased from < 1 to 70% (ibid.). Meanwhile, the Western ideas include "democracy" flourished into China. According to a nationwide survey in 1987, 75% of Chinese were tolerant of the inflow of Western ideas, and 80% of Chinese Communist Party members held a similar attitude (Min 1989, p. 128). Moreover, due to the fast-growing economy, the desire of Chinese intellectuals for the democratization of China became intense. They believed that it was the traditional culture of China hindered the country's democratization and the future of China depended on the thorough westernization (Su et al. 1988). The Chinese nationalists' statue of the "Goddess of Democracy" during Beijing Spring in 1989 tells of their desire for promoting the construction of democracy in China (Gries 2004, p. 6).

The 1989 movement for democratization didn't succeed. For Chinese leaders, the purpose of political reform was not to weaken the Party but to stabilize it (Zheng 1999, p. 50). And the 1989 movement caused a return to the exercises and excesses of sovereign power. The sustained economic development in the 1990s began to satisfy Chinese individual's needs. During this stage, Chinese nationalistic sentiments were shaped both top-down and bottom-up. After the Tiananmen Incident in 1989, especially after Jiang Zemin took over power in 1992, nationalism was promoted as a dominant discourse in China and it was in this era Chinese nationalism turned back to its anti-Western sentiment.

It was argued that the CCP's promotion of nationalism as a new ideology was due to several reasons, that include the collapse of European communism, the reflection on Western culture in China, and the mismatch between a changing society and an old ideology (Zheng 1999, pp. 51–52). First of all, what happened in the Soviet Union and Eastern Europe influenced the thinking of Chinese intellectuals on the traditional ideology. As Sun Liping writes,

> Chinese intellectuals believe that social disintegration is a more serious threat to China than social stagnation and conservatism, that political and social chaos will follow the decline of the traditional ideology and the worsening of social crises. Therefore, it was necessary to promote nationalism as a new ideology (Sun 1996, p. 17, translated in Zheng 1999, p. 51).

Second, Chinese intellectuals started to take a critical approach in receiving the information about the West. While they believed China had to go through thorough Westernization before 1989, the Western impact was considered "negative" on Chinese traditional culture in the 1990s. Also, the West's intentions towards the rise of China were also questioned by Chinese, particularly when the West imposed high conditions on China's entry into the World Trade Organization (Sun 1996, p. 17). Third, the old ideology has become outdated in China since the beginning of the reform and opening up in 1978. A new ideological tool was needed to manage the changing society, and nationalism was the best candidate (Chen 1996, p. 74).

Interestingly, Chinese nationalists in this phase appear to be fond of the "victimization" narrative of the "Century of Humiliation" (Gries 2004, p. 4). They question the inflow of the Western culture that started flooding into China in late 1990s. In 1997, Song Qiang, the author of the aforementioned 2009 nationalistic book *Unhappy China* reflected on the materialism of his generation: "cultural and spiritual fast food has taken over" (Gries 2004, p. 4). This generation believes they are the defenders of China's stability whereas the generation before 1989 is dangerously romantic and radical (Gries 2004, p. 5). An illustrative example here is the "May 8th" nationalist protests of 1999: the demonstration with a painting of the skeleton of the statue of liberty which was in sharp contrast with the 1989s "Goddess of Democracy".

However, it is very important to note that although Chinese nationalists demonstrated their resentment to the Western liberty in this era, the desire for democracy still existed. What were resisted by Chinese nationalists were the Western model of democratization and the Western theories of development. They believed Westernization was the cause of China's national and cultural identity crises, thus, China's modernization should be separated from Westernization, and the future development of China relies on "Chinesenization" rather than Westernization (Zheng 1999, p. 53).

However, the anti-Westernization narrative started to change after 2001 with the rising of China's post-80s generation and with the inspiring achievements China made in 2001 when Beijing was elected for the 2008 Olympic host city, Shanghai hosted APEC, China successfully joined the WTO, and China's national football team got a pass to the World Football Cup for the first time in China's history. This first year of the twenty-first century was called "Chinese year" and seen as a very good sign of China in the new century (China Economic Net 2012). The issue of China's "national and cultural identity crises" due to Westernization expressed by the previous wave of nationalism was gradually replaced by this new wave's pride and "victor narrative".

The resurgence of Chinese nationalism after 2001 presented by Chinese young generation which has drawn the biggest attention around the world in 2008, demonstrated something powerful and different from the previous nationalists. This included the overwhelming extreme pride in the country and its central government. More distinctively, the inflow of Western "cultural and spiritual fast food" that was questioned by the previous generation of nationalists is beloved by this young generation. The anti-West ideology has shifted from entirely anti/pro-Western to the young nationalists' paradoxical feelings of the West, which are the extreme embrace of Western culture while sharply resenting to the Western political ideologies, as described in this chapter.

The Internet as a tool of expression for this generation's nationalistic sentiments has become a distinguishing feature of this wave, because this generation is the first generation to grow up with the Internet in China. While the consumerist ideology dominates the Internet and is represented largely through the young generation's online behaviors as discussed in this chapter, the passion for political issues that involves China's image is also spread and strengthened via the Internet.

The 2008 anti-CNN campaign introduced in Chap. 1 is an illustrative example of the latest Chinese nationalistic sentiment. While high emotions were expressed in the anti-CNN forum after CNN's coverage on Tibet and other Western coverage on Olympic torch relay in 2008, young Chinese also expressed their love for China to support Beijing's Olympic Games via MSN messenger. They added a symbol of red heart to their MSN names and placed the English word "China" next to the red heart. The consistent action of expressing "love China" via MSN was in order to oppose the Western media's coverage over the Beijing Olympic Games protests. It is the representation of Chinese national identity by means of Internet—the resentment of the West and the extreme pride of China—which distinguishes this latest wave of Chinese nationalism from its predecessors. The current first lady of China, President Xi's celebrity wife, Li Yuan Peng's elegant and stylish global appearances have also strengthened this type of "China pride," because she is seen as the best first lady image China ever had. The intimate titles "Xi Da Da" and "Peng Ma Ma" for President Xi and his wife given by Chinese netizens show clearly how they are deeply loved.

2.6   CONCLUSION

James Grunig (2009) argues in favor of two-way communication and highlights the significance social media can have on this dialogic communication. He states that social media used to its full potential can provide public relations with a more two-way and interactive, global, strategic, and socially responsible approach. However, the practice of Foreign Embassies' two-way communication on Weibo has illustrated the impossibility of using social media to fufil these goals. Although Grunig's global public relations theory suggests that practice in different countries should be different based on culture, political system, economic system, media system, level of economic development, and extent and nature of activism in a certain country. But elements like the existence of China's nationalistic sentiments online pose a great obstacle in implementing a two-way systematic communication. It is arguable that a one-way communication approach might work better in some contexts. This book aims to be one of the pioneer books that provide empirical data to explore these theories further.

REFERENCES

BBC. (2008, September 24). Du naifen: "Bu neng" haishi "bu wei" [Poisoned milk powder: "Can't" or "don't"']. http://news.bbc.co.uk/chinese/simp/hi/newsid_7630000/newsid_7634000/7634058.stm. Viewed on 2 April 2009.

Chan, M. K. (1994). From anti-foreignism to popular nationalism: Hong Kong between China and Britain, 1839–1911. In M. K. Chan (Ed.), *Precarious balance: Hong Kong between China and Britain* (pp. 1842–1992). Hong Kong: Hong Kong University Press.

Chang, J. (2003). *Wild swans: Three daughters of China*. Austin: Touchstone.

Chang, J., & Halliday, J. (2005). *Mao: The unknown story*. London: Jonathan Cape.

Chen, S. M. (1996). Min zu zhu yi: Fu xing zhi dao? [Nationalism: a way for revival?]. *DF 2*, 74–76.

China Economic Net. (2012). Australian companies registered Weibo accounts for business opportunities. *China Economics Net*. Retrieved from http://intl.ce.cn/specials/zxgjzh/201203/30/t20120330_23202373.shtml.

CNNIC. (2013). The 31st statistical report on internet development. *CNNIC*. Retrieved February 28, 2014, from http://www1.cnnic.cn/AU/SocialR/SocialNews/201301/t20130121_38607.htm.

Dashan, D. S. (2012). What is weibo? *Quora*. Retrieved from http://www.quora.com/What-is-Weibo.

Dean, M. (1991). *The constitution of poverty: Toward a genealogy of liberal governance*. New York: Routledge.

Deibert, R. (2002). Dark guests and great firewalls: the Internet and Chinese security policy. *Journal of Social Issues, 58*(1), 143–159.

Dillon, M. (Ed.). (1998). *China: A historical and cultural dictionary*. London: Routledge.

Dittmer, L., & Kim, S. (1993). Whither China's quest for national identity? In L. Dittmer, & S. Kim (Eds.), *China's quest for national identity*. Ithaca, NY: Cornell University Press.

Faina, J. (2012). Twitter and the new publicity. *ETC: A Review Of General Semantics, 69*(1), 55–71.

Ford, E. (2013). Billionaire blogger Charles Xue arrested on sex charges in Beijing. *The Times*. Retrieved August 26, 2013, from http://www.thetimes.co.uk/tto/news/world/asia/article3852306.ece.

Grant, W. J., Moon, B., & Busby Grant, J. (2010). Digital dialogue? Australian politicians' use of the social network tool Twitter. *Australian Journal of Political Science, 45*(4), 579–604.

Gries, P. H. (2004). *Chinese new nationalism: Pride, politics, and diplomacy.* Berkeley: University of California Press.

Grunig, J. E. (2009). Paradigms of global public relations in an age of digitalisation. *PRism, 6*(2). http://praxis.massey.ac.nz/prism_on-line_journ.html.

Hsu, I. (1960). *China's entrance into the family of nations: The diplomatic phase, 1858–1880.* Cambridge, MA: Harvard University Press.

Hwang, S. (2012). The strategic use of Twitter to manage personal public relations. *Public Relations Review, 12*, 90–92.

Hu, J. (2002, November 27). Rights group looks at China and tech. *CNET News.* Retrieved March 31, 2009, from http://news.cnet.com/Rights-group-looks-at-China-and-techs/2100-1023_3-975517.html.

Ihlen. (2008). Mapping the environment for corporate social responsibility: Stakeholders, publics and the public sphere. *Corporate Communications, 13*(2), p.142.

Jensen, I. (2001). Public relations and emerging functions of the public sphere: An analytical framework. *Journal of Communication Management, 6*(2), 133–147.

Jiang, Y. (2012). *Cyber-nationalism in China: Challenging western portrayal of Chinese censorship.* Adelaide: University of Adelaide Press.

Kanter, B., & Fine, A. H. (2010). *The networked nonprofit.* San Fransisco, CA: Wiley.

Kluver, A. R. (1996). *Legitimating the Chinese economic reforms: A rhetoric of myth and orthodoxy.* New York: SUNY Press.

Levenson, J. L. (1964). *Modern China and its confucian past: The problem of intellectual continuity.* New York: Anchor Books.

Leichty, G. (1997). The limits of collaboration. *Public Relations Review, 23*(1), 47–55.

Liang, Q. (1959). *Xinmin shuo (on new citizenship).* Taipei: Zhonghua Shuju.

Liang, Q. (1989a). 'Zhongguoshi xulun' (A narrative analysis of Chinese history). In Q. Liang (Eds.), *Yinbingshi heji,* (Vol. 1, p. 3). Beijing: Zhongguo Shuju.

Liang, Q. (1989b). 'Zhongguo liguo zhi dafangzhen' (The fundamental policies for China's being a nation-state). In Q. Liang (Eds.), *Yinbingshi heji,* (Vol. 4, pp. 39–78). Beijing: Zhongguo Shuju.

Lin, Y. (1979). *The crisis of Chinese consciousness.* Madison: The University of Wisconsin Press.

Mackinnon, R. (2009, February 2). China's censorship 2.0: How companies censor bloggers. *First Monday14*(2),http://firstmonday.org/htbin/cgiwrap/bin/ojs/index.php/fm/article/view/2378/2089, Viewed on 23 June 2009.

Marwick, A., & Boyd, D. (2012). To see and be seen: celebrity practice on Twitter. *Convergence: The Journal of Research into New Media Technologies*, 17, 139–158.

McNaughton, M. (2012, January 6). Developing countries see rapid social networking growth. http://therealtimereport.com/2012/01/06/developing-countries-see-rapid-social-networking-growth/.

Min, Q. (1989). *Zhongguo zhengzhi wenhua* [Political culture in China]. Kunming: Unnan Renmin C1hubanshe.

Murphy, P. (1991). The limits of symmetry: A game theory approach to symmetrical and asymmetrical public relations. In L. A. Grunig & J. E. Grunig (Eds.), *Public relations research annual* (Vol. 3, pp. 115–131). Hillsdale, NJ: Lawrence Erlbaum Associates, Inc.

Pan, P. (2006, February 18). Keywords used to filter web content. *Washington Post*. http://www.washingtonpost.com/wp-dyn/content/article/2006/02/18/AR2006021800554.html, Viewed 14 April 2009.

Pasadeos, Y., Berger, B., & Renfro, B. (2010). Public relations as a maturing discipline: An update on research networks. *Journal of Public Relations Research*, 22(2), 136–158. doi:10.1080/10627261003601390.

Phillips, D., & Young, P. (2009). *Online public relations: A practical guide to developing an online strategy in the world of social media* (2nd ed.). London: Kogan Page Limited.

Porter, J. (2009). Relationship symmetry in social networks: Why Facebook will go fully asymmetric. *Bokard*. Retrieved February, 28 from http://bokardo.com/archives/relationship-symmetry-on-social-networks-why-facebook-will-go-fullu-asymmetric/.

Raymond, E. (1999). The cathedral and the bazaar. *Knowledge, Technology & Policy, 12*, 23–49.

Schwartz, B. (1964). *In search of wealth and power*. New York: Harper Torchbook.

Su, X. K., et al. (1988). *Heshang [River Elegy]*. Beijing: Xian dai chu ban she.

Sun, L. P. (1996). Huiru shijie zhuliu wenming-minzu zhuyi santi [Flowing together with the world's mainstream civilization]. *DF 1*, 15–19.

Tai, Z. (2006). *The internet in China: cyberspace and civil society*. London: Routledge.

Teiwes, F. C. (1996). Seeking the historical Mao. *The China Quarterly 145*(March), 176–188.

Tsui, L. (2001). *Big mama is watching you: Internet control by the Chinese government*. Unpublished MA. thesis, University of Leiden, Leiden.

Tyson, A. (1995). *Chinese awakenings: Life stories from the unofficial China*. Boulder, CO: Westview Press.

Wang, G. W. (1996). *The revival of Chinese nationalism*. Leiden: International Institute for AsianStudies.

Wang, K. W. (Ed.). (1998). *Modern China: An encyclopedia of history, culture, and nationalism.* New York: Garland Publishing.

Wei, C. X. G., & Liu, X. Y. (2001). *Chinese nationalism in perspective: Historical and recent cases.* Lanham, MD: Greenwood Publishing Group.

Wei, C. X. G., Liu, X. Y., & Kirby, W. C. (2002). *Exploring nationalisms of China: Themes and conflicts.* Lanham, MD: Greenwood Publishing Group.

Weiquan Wang [Chinese Human Rights Defenders]. (2008, July 10). Zhongguo wangluo jiankong yu fanjiankong niandu baogao (2007) [Annual report on Chinese Internet surveillance and actions against surveillance]. http://crd-net.org/Article/Class1/200807/20080710165332_9340.html. Viewed 25 March 2009.

Xiao, Q. (2004, August 30). 'The words you never see in Chinese cyberspace', *China Digital Times.* Retrieved April 15, 2009, from http://chinadigital-times.net/2004/08/the_words_you_n.php.

Xiao, Q (2005). The words you never see in Chinese cyberspace, *China Digital Times,* 30 August. Retrieved April 15, 2009, from http://chinadigitaltimes.net/2004/08/the_words_you_n.php.

Yujiro, M. (1997). Dynasty, state, and society: The case of modern China. In J. A. Fogel & P. G. Zarrow (Eds.), *Imagining the people: Chinese intellectual and the concept of citizenship* (pp. 1890–1929). Armonk: M.E. Sharpe.

Zhang, X. D. (2001). *Whither China? Intellectual politics in contemporary China.* Durham, NC: Duke University Press.

Zhao, S. S. (2004). *A nation-state by construction: Dynamics of modern Chinese nationalism.* Stanford, CA: Stanford University Press.

Zheng, Y. N. (1999). *Discovering Chinese nationalism in China: Modernization, identity, and international relations.* Cambridge: Cambridge University Press.

PART II

Analyzing the Embassies' Use of Weibo

CHAPTER 3

Scanning the Foreign Use of Weibo

Abstract This chapter introduces the practice of e-diplomacy on Weibo by foreign embassies in Beijing. The key aim of this chapter is to bring an overall picture of foreign use of Weibo and identify the top five embassies that use Weibo frequently. It seeks to address three gaps in existing knowledge by empirical research. Firstly, at present, we simply do not know—in a systematic sense—what foreign embassies are doing on Weibo. We do not know which embassies have the most followers on Weibo, how often they Weibo, and what they are posting about. Secondly, this chapter seeks to address the fact that we do not have a clear understanding of the benefit that foreign embassies are gaining from the Chinese online platform. It is not clear that what these benefits are due to their Weibo behavior. Finally, this chapter seeks to address the deeper question: what the uptake of foreign embassy users of Chinese social media—and Chinese Weibo in particular—means for public diplomacy. Does Weibo offer better ways for public diplomacy workers to communicate with potential audience, or is it instead a fragmentary, dangerous, and disempowering distraction?

Keywords Chinese social media · Weibo · Public diplomacy

© The Author(s) 2017
Y. Jiang, *Social Media and e-Diplomacy in China*,
DOI 10.1057/978-1-137-59358-0_3

3.1   INTRODUCTION

Social media is one of the fastest growing tools of modern public diplomacy. It is arguable that the perceived ease with which social media can be accessed and the low cost in comparison to other methods make it an attractive tool for many embassies and other organizations (Fisher 2013). For those organizations who are facing budget cuts and demand to increase engagement, social media seems to be an ideal communication tool.

President Obama's campaign use of Web 2.0 social media platforms, such as Facebook, Twitter, and YouTube, is arguably the largest contributing factor to its success in 2008 (Harris 2014). Since Obama's use of Web 2.0 as a strategy to win the 2008 presidential election, social media has been used as a tool to cultivate relations between the government and the individual—essentially democratizing government communications (Cogburn and Espinoza-Vasquez 2011, p. 191). With "21 million registered members and 1.6 billion page views each day," Obama was able to gain political support through a hybrid strategy, which took advantage of both Web 2.0 and social media tools (Cogburn and Espinoza-Vasquez 2011, p. 191).

As Harris argues, Web 2.0's value as a tool in domestic politics is easily transferrable to foreign politics (Harris 2013). The US has become more involved abroad and has augmented its number of diplomatic missions throughout the world. The focus on diplomacy by the Obama administration is a first step toward improvement in the overall American brand (Harris 2013). Engagement is an important part of diplomacy and using social media is one way to promote a positive image, because social media provides the right channel to reach youth populations (Merson 2012). To reach out the young generation is one of the major goals of current public diplomacy efforts. For public diplomacy, it is equally important to listen to and understand young populations' thoughts, aspirations, information seeking, and other behaviors (Riordan 2004). Apart from reaching a youth audience, social media platforms also provide spaces for interaction, increased engagement, and thus furthering the goals of public diplomacy.

There has been limited research addressing the question of whether it is useful to use social media by foreign embassies. Research on the usefulness of Weibo by embassies was not found. For those countries who have decided to embark on a Chinese social media platform, are they conversing or simply broadcasting themselves? Is the existence of embassies' Weibo accounts providing a more effective tool for reaching citizens, and encouraging more interactive engagement? What benefits have Weibo brought to embassies in China? This empirical research aims to answer these above questions.

This chapter seeks to address three gaps in existing knowledge by empirical research. Firstly, at present, we simply do not know—in a systematic sense—what foreign embassies are doing on Weibo. We do not know which embassies have the most followers on Weibo, how often they Weibo, and what they are posting about.

Secondly, this chapter seeks to address the fact that we do not have a clear understanding of the benefit that foreign embassies are gaining from the Chinese online platform. It is not clear that what these benefits are due to their Weibo behavior.

Finally, this chapter seeks to address the deeper question: what the uptake of foreign embassy users of Chinese social media—and Chinese Weibo in particular—means for public diplomacy. Does Weibo offer better ways for public diplomacy workers to communicate with potential audience, or is it instead a fragmentary, dangerous, and disempowering distraction?

3.2   BACKGROUND

3.2.1   Brief Overview of Social Media and Public Diplomacy

Social media is one of the fastest growing tools of modern public diplomacy. Social media provides the right channel to reach youth populations, which is one of the major goals of current public diplomacy efforts. Researchers have started paying attention to social media and public relations/diplomacy in recent years, for example, in New Media and Public Diplomacy in Network Society, Jordi Xifra analyzes the role of new media and social media in public relations and focuses on nation-building (Xifra 2012). Xifra and Grau (2010) found that Twitter discourse related to public relations contributed more to practice than theory. Smith (2010) observed that communication power was shifting away from public relations practitioners to social media users whose organizational interests or roles may not be well defined, he suggests, this results "a social model of public relations in which traditional public relations responsibilities are distributed to social media users" (Smith

2010, p. 329). In his work, Smith emphasized that "scholars move beyond efforts to simply translate public relations models into online sphere ... consider this an opportunity to consider new levels of risk, relationship, and interactivity" (p. 334).

According to the Public Relations Society of America, "public relations is a strategic communication public diplomacy also uses strategic communication to improve perceptions of a country to foreign publics" (PRSA 2013). Since public diplomacy also uses strategic communication to improve perceptions of a country to foreign publics, these areas of communications are often related. Beata Ociepka argues that traditional forms of public diplomacy are related to propaganda and prevents PD initiatives from being seen as ethical (Ociepka 2012). Therefore, PD initiatives have suffered due to the negative perception that public relations and propaganda are always related. However, Ociepka suggests that the addition of social media to PD strategies has added to the engagement potential for PD initiatives.

Research on the government application of new media has a long existence. In 1985, Harris, Garramone, Pizante, and Komiya were the first to discuss how computers could provide a two-way flow of information between elected officials and their constituents. McKeown and Plowman (1999) explained how 1996 US presidential candidates used the Web to reach voters during the general election, Trammell (2006) explained how blog-based attacks were utilized during the 2004 US election; Levenshus's (2010) article explained how Obama campaign utilized the Internet for grassroots efforts in 2008. Other scholars looked at how Middle East and UAE governmental organizations used the Internet (Curtin and Gaither 2004; Ayish 2005; Kirat 2007), as well as the role of culture in country-sponsored tourism websites (Kang and Mastin 2008), the diffusion of social media in public health communication (Avery et al. 2010), and the impact of transparency laws on Latin American government websites (Searson and Johnson 2010).

Public diplomacy generally refers to "a government's process of communicating with foreign publics in an attempt to bring about understanding for its nation's ideas and ideals, its institutions and culture, as well as its national goals and current policies" (Tuch 1990, p. 3). Traditionally, public diplomacy has been understood in terms of the relation between one nation-state and its foreign publics, that nation's main objective being to cultivate a favorable image of itself on the world stage. However, a young and multidisciplinary area, public diplomacy is often criticized for a paucity of theoretical grounding and the tools necessary to attract and persuade foreign publics.

Signitzer and Coombs (1992) identify conceptual conversion between public diplomacy and public relations because public diplomacy and public relations have similar aims of affecting public opinion to benefit their client or organization. Public relations is often studied and practiced as relationship management (Broom et al. 1997; Ferguson 1984; Ledingham and Bruning 1998, 2000). Public diplomacy, described as "the actual communication activity by a political entity" (Zaharna 2010, p. 79), may be perceived as a form of international public relations insofar as it also involves relationship management and public relations tactics intended to effect change in foreign public.

Social media use can add to the policy-making process, as its tools can provide a platform for symmetrical communication (Ociepka 2012, p. 59). Symmetrical communication is "allowing individuals to intensify social contacts while sharing content, engaging in discussion, but also controlling content via networks they participate in" (ibid). Using social media has enabled political entities to engage in branding and promoting a specific persona to their audiences. According to Harris (2013), social media are effective for conveying any message to a given public, whether it is from a corporation, a public figure, or a government. The use of social media in politics has been an effective tool in garnering public support and thus provides strategic utility in the practice of public diplomacy.

3.2.2   Social Media Platforms Used by Embassies in the US

Research analyzing the use of social media platforms to accomplish foreign policy objectives existed, and Hayden found that social media proved effective in influencing public opinion as a public relations tool in Obama's 2008 campaign (Hayden 2011). Therefore, it is impossible to accomplish any foreign policy objective requiring cooperation of civilians in a country when the local population is opposed to the foreign nation's presence (Chavez and Hoewe 2010). In the case of Mexico, social media can be an effective and strategic tool of PD initiatives because the country as a whole has adequate access to the Internet and some social media sites (ibid). These sites can be used to distribute information internationally; however, it is important that the information is available in both

Spanish and English, which allows for active participation by citizens and governments (ibid).

In "Practicing Successful Twitter Public Diplomacy: A model and case study of US efforts in Venezuela," Yepsen designs her research to create a model where the US Embassy in Venezuela could successfully attempt Twitter diplomacy (Yepsen 2012). According to Yepsen, an embassy needs to limit the topics it covers, using Twitter to centralize discussion and "identify the ideal network"(ibid, p. 20). By using websites such as TwitterHolic and RetweetRank, Yepsen identified users in Venezuela who have more followers and the potential to influence a substantial amount of people based on a high volume of retweets (ibid, p. 22). Yepsen identified six Venezuelan users who appeared at the top of 1000 most followed users: @chavezcandanga (President Hugo Chavez), @ElUniversal (a newspaper), @la_ patilla (an "information and investigation" website), @globovision (a television news channel), @Noticias24 (a news website), and @LuisChataing (an actor and television personablity) (ibid) These Twitter users were determined as an ideal target because the large amount of followers would ensure exposure if US Embassy content was retweeted (ibid).

Yepsen expanded the list of six to "all users who were replied to or retweeted at least 10 times by one of the leaders" (ibid). By setting a threshold of 30% for "diversified interests and relationship maintenance tweets," Yepsen was able to set a "satisfactory limit to ensure content would be worth the public diplomat's time while still allowing for opinion leaders with other topical interests to be included" (ibid). After analyzing the six original leaders, @LuisChataing was eliminated based on the 30% threshold requirement (ibid). Of the 100 leaders selected, only 30 leaders met the threshold and were selected to be part of the study. To strengthen the level of potential influence of the sample, Yepsen included retweet strength as a criterion and increased the number of individual networks and account holders to 47, including the US Embassy in Venezuela (ibid). These 47 networks were ranked based on their networking capabilities (number of networks that can be made) and their follower strength (ibid). Yepsen narrowed the list based on rank to the top 30 Twitter users including the US Embassy (ibid). After further research, Yepsen discovered that the US Embassy has restrictions placed on political content posted on Twitter. Therefore, the US Embassy focuses more on cultural aspects when tweeting and deletes "partisan tweets" (ibid). Yepsen determined that an ideal network does exist if the US Embassy wanted to get involved in discussion about US—Venezuelan foreign policy issues.

Current scholarship agrees that social media sites, particularly Twitter, are important tools in enhancing PD practices (Harris 2013). PD as a practice has developed a negative reputation, much like public relations, because of the traditional asymmetrical, top-down flow of information, which has dominated the practice (Taylor 2007). While analyzing tweets by governmental organizations, it is apparent that Twitter provides a platform where not only is asymmetrical information possible, but symmetrical information is possible too (Harris 2013). Traditional forms of media provide a top-down flow of information, as those in power within the organization have the greatest potential to have their perspectives and information published in the paper and broadcast on the news. However, Smith argues that as evidenced in the case of the Haitian earthquake in 2010, social media allow civilians to have the power to control and distribute information (Smith 2010). Furthermore, the use of social media in times of crisis by a US Embassy can garner public support for a US presence, as it did in Japan. Foreign civilians need to know the US has a vested interest in their well-being. As a result, broadcasting accurate information in times of crisis and listening to the concerns of people abroad will create a level of trust. When trust is created and people feel connected to the US message, people who are active on Twitter will be more willing to risk their reputations within their network to broadcast that message (ibid).

In 2013, systematic research specifically focuses on the use of social media by embassies started to make its appearance. One of the worth mentioning project is the Global Communication program, which is joint venture between the Elliott School of International Affairs and the School of Media and Public Affairs at George Washington University. In this program, Dr. Fisher and his team look at the uses of e-diplomacy by foreign embassies in the US.

With over 170 diplomatic missions in the US, American citizens and social media users around the world have a vast range of channels with which to engage. Adding to the range of channels, many embassies also have multiple accounts on the same platform, often an account representing the Ambassador and an account for the embassy. Dr. Ali Fisher found that every embassy in DC, that uses more than one platform, uses at least one of Facebook or Twitter as part of their e-diplomacy strategy.

Some embassies will use more than one platform to conduct e-diplomacy (Fig. 3.1).

However, this capstone project didn't deal with some in-depth questions, such as which embassies are reaching the most users? Which Ambassadors or representatives are reaching the most users? Are embassies using the persona of an 'Ambassador' more frequently than 'Embassy' accounts? Do the same social media users engage with both an Ambassador and Embassy from the same country?

3.2.3   Social Media Platforms in China

The social media landscape in China is very different from the rest of the world. A brief summary of the history of Chinese social media is of importance to more fully understand the unique and complex Chinese social media landscape. The first bulletin board system (BBS) was built in 1994 and Chinese netizens quickly began to engage within online forums and communities; one such example was the famous BBS *Xicihutong* (*xici.net*). In the beginning of the 1990s, computers were luxury products to the ordinary people of China—there were few Internet users (He and Pedraza-Jimenez 2015).

The real Internet boom in China began with the emergence of instant messaging (IM) with *QQ*, which was launched by *Tencent* in 1999. Millions of young people and college students started to chat with friends, or to make new friends, via the *QQ* platform, which was similar to *ICQ* (I seek you) (ibid). *BlogChina* (*blogchina.com*), another revolutionary tool, was released in 2002 by founder *Fangxingdong*. In addition to *IMing*, Chinese netizens were enthusiastic about blogging, social network sites (SNS), microblogging platforms, and other social media applications. Relevant examples include the attractive social networking service *Kaixinwang* (*kaixin001.com*) in 2008; the popular microblogging channel *Sina Weibo* (*d.weibo.com*) in 2009; the convenient location-based service (LBS) *Jiepang* (*jiepang.com*) and group buying site *Meituan* (*meituan.com*) in 2010; and the fascinating mobile app *Wechat* platform (*Weixin* in China) in 2011.

Nowadays, Chinese digital users normally have several social media accounts and integrate blogging, SNS, microblogging, online picture sharing, and online video sharing. In fact, not only the normal Internet users, but also the professional news websites (for example: *People's daily*) are accustomed to utilizing local social media applications to meet their

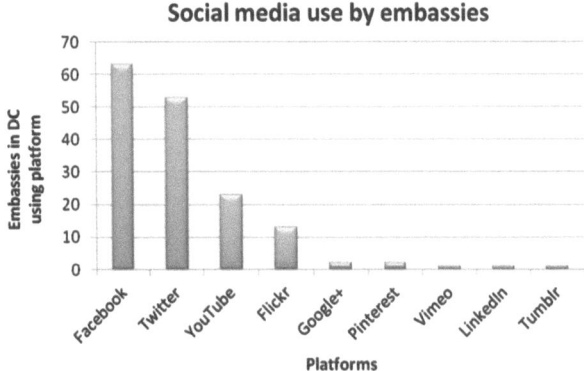

Fig. 3.1 Social media use by embassies in DC. *Source* http://takefiveblog.
org/2013/02/19/the-use-of-social-media-in-public-diplomacy-scanning-e-di-
plomacy-by-embassies-in-washington-dc/

needs (Lim 2014). The landscape of Chinese social media is continuously undergoing fast-paced changes, and has become a rich and diverse
ecosystem of social media. Currently, social media in China is experienc-
ing impressive growth. It is worth mentioning that Chinese social media
applications are not copies of their Western equivalents, but instead they
are new creations that have been innovated to meet Chinese netizens'
habits and behavior, even if they were initially built based on some functions and characteristics of their Western counterparts (Sullivan 2014).
Today, some Chinese social media innovations are even leading the
global trend of social media development. For example, *Weixin* (similar
to *WhatsApp*) offers multiple features such as voice and text messaging,
shaking the handset to look for friends, as well as a social networking
function with the name *WeChat friends*. The interesting features of this
application have led some experts to consider it better than *WhatsApp*.
Information about this leadership of Chinese platforms can be found
even in the Spanish newspaper *El pais* (Aldama 2013). As a result, China
is becoming one of the most active players in the social media world.
The following table (Table 3.1) shows some of the most popular Chinese
social media platforms alongside their occidental counterparts.

  It should be kept in mind that almost everyone has a *QQ* account
in China and *QQ* is linked to *Qzone* (*qzone.qq.com*, a social network
similar to *Facebook*). Both *QQ* and *Qzone* belong to *Tencent* holdings.

Table 3.1 Popular Chinese social media platforms with their occidental counterparts

Social media types	Chinese social media platforms	Occidental counterparts
Microblogging	Sina Weibo; Tecent Weibo	Twitter
Social network sites	Qzone; Renren; Kaixin; WeChat friends	Facebook
Video sharing sites	Youku; Tudou	YouTube
Photo sharing sites	Bababian; Babidou	Flickr
Instant messaging	QQ	MSN
Q&A	Tianya Wenda; Baidu Zhidao	Answers
Wikis	Hudong Baike; Baidu Baike	Wikipedia
LBS	Jiepang	Foursquare

Source He and Pedraza-Jimenez (2015)

In this way, *Qzone* bears a significant user base. In addition, other top social networks in China include *Kaixin* and *Renren*. And the top two social media platforms are *Weixin* (355 million monthly active users) and *Sina Weibo* (129 million monthly active users) (Xu 2014). In general, the Chinese social media ecosystem is very special and different from its counterparts in other countries. In fact, these platforms "live" in a complicated, competitive, and quick-changing environment. It is standard in China for every social media platform to have several "brands" that belong to different companies. All Chinese social media tools are designed and built by local corporations. Therefore, China's social media landscape has the following characteristics: unique, complex, fragmented, and local.

To summarize, while Facebook, Twitter, and Linkedin are regarded as the top three social media platforms in the world, none of these three are available in China due to the country's Internet regulations. Instead, the three most popular social media in China are: Sina Weibo, Tencent Weibo, and Renren Net. They will be introduced respectively in the following paragraphs.

As introduced in the opening section, Weibo is a Chinese microblogging (Weibo) website, in use by well over 30% of the world's Internet users, with a similar market penetration that Twitter has established in the US. Although the most recent CNNIC (China Internet Network Information Center) report in December 2012 announced that there are

309 million Weibo users in China (CNNIC 2013); the announced numbers of Weibo users provided by each Weibo service providers are much higher than the figure this official report disclosed. This is probably due to the competition between each Weibo service providers, but scholars and journalists in China often use the estimation of more than 400 million, which is somewhere between CNNIC's official report and commercial Weibo service providers statistics.

It is important to note that, when Chinese people say "Weibo" it is commonly referred to Sina Weibo. However, Sina Weibo is just one of the various Weibo service competitors. Sina Weibo claims that it has around 500 million registered accounts as of December 2012 (Gao 2013). Others include Tencent (the owner of QQ.com) which also alleged having a microblog site with 400 million registered accounts; and Sohu Weibo with over 100 million registered accounts (Business in Asia.com 2012). Therefore, it is more accurate to say "Tencent Weibo (Tenxun Weibo)" and "Sohu Weibo (Souhu Weibo)" to differentiate from "Sina Weibo (Xinlang Weibo)".

Due to its success of overseas users' penetration, Sina Weibo is still the most well-known Weibo service; therefore, the term Weibo used in this article refers to Sina Weibo.

Weibo, similar to Twitter, is more "conversational" than many other social media platforms. Weibo users can use 140 characters to share what's happening with others. The core element of Weibo is based on the model of human relations (Porter 2009). One doesn't need to become friends with others to be able to read each other's posts. One might follow 10,000 users while only 50 users follow oneself; one might only follow five users but having 10,000 users following one's own account.

China has Renren Net equivalent to Facebook in the West; neither of them allows "conversation" between non-friends. So if Renren and Facebook are viewed as a lounge room in someone's house, Weibo and Twitter would be a bar or street plaza, because anyone who is interested in the topic can join the conversation despite whether you follow each other (Raymond 1999; Grant et al. 2010). Therefore, Weibo and Twitter are closer to a public space, and have unique advantages of becoming effective communication tools for reputation management and community engagement. According to the 2010 statistical results published on WebBizideas.com, 26% of American corporations would pay for business functionality on Twitter (Hwang 2011). Celebrities in the world have also embraced this social media to gather more "followers" (Faina 2012; Marwick and Boyd 2011).

Weibo like Twitter, restrict posts to a maximum of 140 characters. However, it is over simplistic to define Weibo as "Chinese versions of Twitter". Both Sina Weibo and Tencent Weibo are providing more complex and advanced services than Twitter, for example, allowing users to add comments when retweet, whereas Twitter doesn't allow this function. Due to the blockage of Twitter and Facebook in China, the social media landscape in China is dominated by domestic brands rather than these international big names. Chinese domestic companies such as Sina and Tencent are intent on developing more complex hybrids that build on their respective advantages as multifaceted web portals (Dashan 2012). Thus, it would be more accurate to say that Weibo refers to Chinese microblogs that are hybrids of both Twitter and Facebook (Dashan 2012).

Journalists and a handful of scholars in China started paying attention to foreign embassies' use of Weibo (ChinaLabs 2013a, b); however, there has been no systematic study of the effectiveness and challenges of using Weibo for public diplomatic communication. Some scholars started looking at the use of Chinese social media generally, for example, Luo Yi's research examines how public relations practitioners in China use social media for relationship management in China (Luo 2012). Men and Tsai (2012) examined how companies use popular social network sites to facilitate dialogs with publics in China.

But research on the governmental organizations application of Chinese social media is rare. Importantly, when it comes to incidents like the "Kunming terror attack" in China in March 2014, Chinese Weibo users tend to express severe nationalistic sentiments towards foreign countries' statements, and those Weibo accounts of foreign embassies became targets. Those nationalistic comments left on foreign embassies' Weibo pages, mainly criticizing those embassies' "soft statements", have caused the difficulties of e-diplomacy and are calling for immediate attention (Tang 2014).

3.3   Key Research Questions

- Which social media platforms are used to conduct e-diplomacy in China by foreign embassies?
- Which platforms are embassies most frequently using to conduct e-diplomacy in China?

- Which embassies are reaching the most users?
- For those embassies who have decided to embark on a Chinese social media platform, are they conversing or simply broadcasting themselves?
- Is the existence of embassies' Weibo accounts providing a more effective tool for reaching citizens, and encouraging more active engagement?

3.4   METHODS

To address these above issues, I first gathered a list of embassies on Chinese social media platforms. For the purpose of this study, the definition of an embassy's Chinese social media account refers to the embassy's official account that's verified by the service provider. It doesn't include any ambassdor's personal account. It doesn't include any consular or consular staff's account.

To gather this list, I mainly used one simple method: trawling for known embassies through Sina Weibo's celebrity plaza (Mingren Tang), where embassies are categorized by their countries. Following this, I then gathered a list of Foreign embassy Weibo users. Numerical and descriptive data (self-written Twitter biography, representative avatar, number of friends, and number of followers) were collected for each of our examined Weibo users. Further descriptive data (country and registered date) were collected and archived with both text and time/date tweeted. In order to analyze a similar series of tweets, this was then edited to a 3-month period between March and June 2015. Echoing the method of Leavitt and colleagues (Leavitt et al. 2009), I then categorized each of the Weibo posts in the 3-month sample as one of our four basic types: "broadcast," "broadcast mention," "reply," and "retweet." Here, a "broadcast" tweet is an isolated statement without reference to any other Weibo or Weibo user. A "broadcast mention" is also an isolated statement, but one which mentions another Weibo user. A "reply" Weibo is a reply to the post of another Weibo user, with that user listed at the start of the tweet. Finally, a "retweet" is the quoting and re-posting of another user's Weibo in order to pass that Weibo on, usually in the form "RT @username text." These were collectively treated as either "broadcast" (broadcast + broadcast mention) or "conversational" (reply + retweet).

3.5   RESULTS

3.5.1   General Information Collection

As to 6 June 2015, there are 33 Foreign embassies having Weibo account, 11 Foreign embassies are on Tencent Weibo, 8 of them also run Wechat platform, and 2 of them have Douban accounts (Fig. 3.2). Given that Sina Weibo clearly has the most embassy users; this research has chosen to focus on Sina Weibo. These embassies' names, number of followers, number of followings, and number of posts are categorized as below (See Table 3.2).

Based on the data collected during this research, Canada has the most followers on Sina Weibo. Canada's followers has surpassed the US and reached more than 1.1 million. US Embassy has around 900,000 followers as to 6 June 2015. Cuba and the UK have same number of followers and ranked 3rd on the list, while Korean Embassy's Sina Weibo followers are slightly less than Cuba and the UK (Fig. 3.3).

3.5.1.1 Top 5 Embassies with Most Tweets

Although Canada has the highest number of followers, it is not the most active foreign embassy account on Sina Weibo. With more than 8000 Weibo tweets, US Embassy has the most tweets. French Embassy's number of Weibo tweets ranks number 2, which is slightly more than Canada. The UK and Denmark have 4000 and 3000 tweets, respectively (Fig. 3.4).

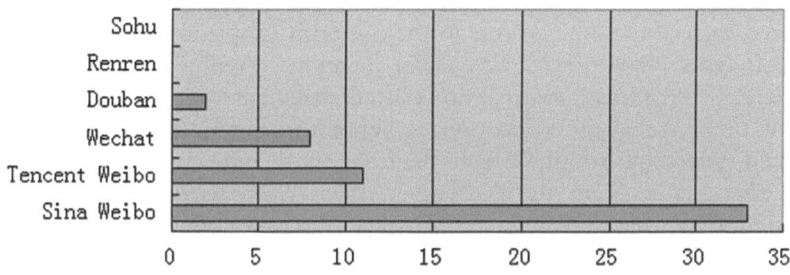

Fig. 3.2 Most popular social media platforms in China. *Source* Author's compilation based on her own research (data updated on 6 June 2015)

Table 3.2 Top 5 embassies with most followers

Country	Canada	US	Cuba	UK	Korea	Japan	France	Russia	Denmark	Australia
Number of followers	1,120,000	900,000	360,000	360,000	330,000	290,000	230,000	140,000	130,000	110,000
Number of following	137	262	52	1035	477	70	691	95	161	55
Number of tweets	4674	8549	417	4070	2947	2807	4866	2370	3037	1416

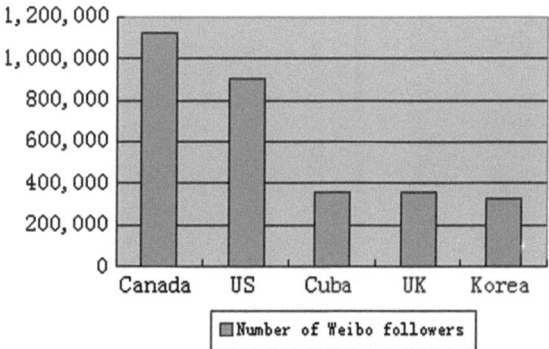

Fig. 3.3 Top 5 embassies with most followers. *Source* Author's compilation based on her own research (data updated on 6 June 2015)

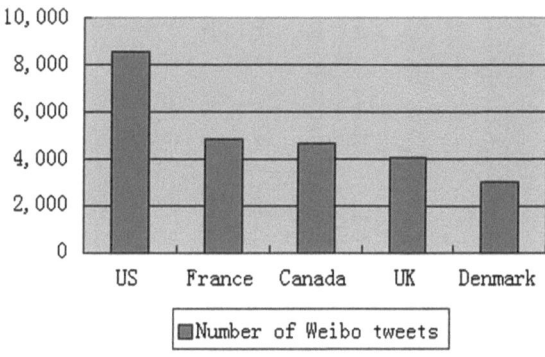

Fig. 3.4 Top 5 embassies with most tweets. *Source* Author's compilation based on her own research (data updated on 6 June 2015)

3.5.2 Statistics on "Conversational" Communication

If we categorize "reply" and "retweet" as conversational, "broadcast" and "mentioning broadcast" as broadcasting, the level of each embassy's conversational communication degree on Weibo can be presented as following. While "broadcasting" posts are the most, US Embassy has more conversational posts than the rest of embassies. But if we look at the ratio

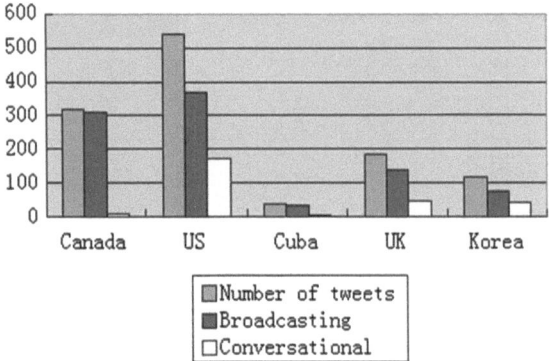

Fig. 3.5 Statistics on "conversational" communication. *Source* Author's compilation based on her own research (data updated on 6 June 2015)

of number of tweets and conversational tweets, Korean Embassy's Weibo account is the most "conversational" one (see Fig. 3.5).

3.5.3   *Statistics on Their Weibo Influence*

The influence of each embassy on Weibo can be assessed by calculating the number of comments on their posts and the number of retweets of their posts. After analyzing the number of comments and retweets each embassy received on their Weibo from March to June in 2013, I have gathered the following results: Korean embassy has the highest ratio of retweets and comments (see Fig. 3.6).

3.6   DISCUSSION

1. Which social media platforms are used to conduct e-diplomacy in China by foreign embassies? Which platforms are embassies most frequently using to conduct e-diplomacy in China?
   Based on the information collected during this research, the top three most used social media platforms in China by foreign embassies are Sina Weibo, Tencent Weibo, and Wechat. The number of foreign embassy accounts on Sina Weibo almost triples the acccounts on Tencent Weibo and four times the accounts on Wechat. However, given Wechat is catching up very fastly in China, and

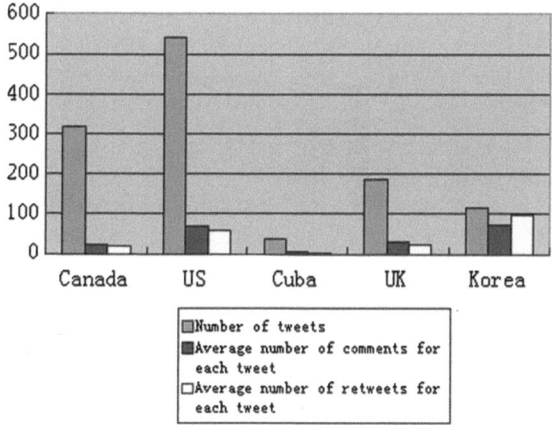

Fig. 3.6 Statistics on embassies' Weibo influence. *Source* Author's compilation based on her own research (data updated on 6 June 2015)

Tencent Weibo is gradually losing its popularity, it is very likely to expect a sharp increase in the use of Wechat by foreign embassies and a significant decrease of using Tencent Weibo in the near future.

2. Which embassies are reaching the most users?

   Based on the data collected during this research, Canada has the most followers on Sina Weibo, the US have the highest number of tweets. However, the number followers do not necessarily equate a strong connection with an audience. An account might have a million followers say nothing, even though a post gets retweeted 1000 times per day, it doesn't indicate whether those followers are supporting or against the user's communication goals.

3. For those embassies who have decided to embark on a Chinese social media platform, are they conversing or simply broadcasting themselves?

   According to the statistics conducted in this research, all the embassies on Sina Weibo have "conversational" tweets. However, the number of "conversational" tweets varies significantly among those embassies. It is evident that Korea, US, and UK embassies attempt to engage interactively with their followers. It is arguable that, Korean embassy has the highest "conversational" communication is mainly because its attractive Korean pop culture content for Weibo users who are mainly young Chinese.

你喜欢看罗宾•威廉姆斯主演的电影吗？你是他的影迷吗？你想和我们一起在欣赏罗宾•威廉姆斯的电影同时开怀大笑吗？十月，北京美国中心将以一部由威廉姆斯出演的"死亡诗社"为开篇回顾罗宾•威廉姆斯。下一部罗宾•威廉姆斯电影回顾将由你来决定！详情：

🔗 网页链接 或 🔗 网页链接

2014-9-30 16.05 来自 微博 weibo.com

| 收藏 | 转发 64 | 评论 538 | 👍66 |

全部 热门 认证用户 关注的人   共538条

胭脂哀：试问揽屎棍哪家强？！同意的顶起来！
2014-9-30 19:16   回复 👍35

九一二Tiger：香港是中国的香港，是中国人民的，没事别瞎BB，不要干涉我国内政，你们国家黑人上街抗议，你们怎么对待的，管好你们自己的"民主"吧！
2014-10-1 09:04   回复 👍41

路边一财狼：美国号称"猎人"的老兵怎么跑到乌克兰去啦？民主？你们怎么回事啊。
2014-9-30 21:30   回复 👍13

抽了个烟的 ★：联合国喊你交会费🐱
2014-10-5 11:36   回复 👍10

尘尘他爸：看到有人骂你我就放心了
2014-10-2 08:24   回复 👍8

胡晗微博 ★：让爱与和平占领白宫！
2014-10-2 12:37   回复 👍6

OvO_拉着喻队四处浪浪浪w：为联合国抹一把辛酸泪 交个会费会死么！
2014-10-2 12:42   回复 👍49

彬小小彬 V：孔子学院停办怎么不转发？
2014-10-3 11:26   回复 👍2

Fig. 3.7   Examples of comments left on US Embassy's Weibo account

4. Is the existence of embassies' Weibo accounts providing a more effective tool for reaching citizens, and encouraging more active engagement?

According to the data collected in this research, it is evident that Weibo can be effective in terms of reaching out citizens. Comparing with conventional offline public diplomacy, reaching out target group via social media is much more cost-effective and efficient. When it comes to encouraging more active engagement, Weibo is also effective. However, based on data collected in this research, active engagement can be negative engagement; the followers can also be citizens who are against a particular country. For example, American embassy has the highest number of followers as well as the highest number of retweets and comments; however, more than half of the comments it received are negative comments that contain nationalistic and hostile content (Fig. 3.7).

3.6.1   Brief Translation:

3.6.1.1 Original Weibo Post by US Embassy

Do you like Robin William's films? Are you a fan of him? Would you like to watch Robin William's movies with us and have fun together? October, Beijing American Center will start memorizing Robin William with one of his movies. The next Robin William movie review will be decided by you.

Comments left by users:

Yanzhiai	Who is the most effective shit mixing stick? Support me if you agree.
Jiuyier Tiger	Hong Kong belongs to China, belongs to Chinese people, stop interfering China's domestic affairs! Take care of your own democracy.
Lubianyicailang	Why your American solider went to Ukrain? What's happening to your democracy?
Choulegeyande	The UN calls you to pay membership fee.
Chenchentaba	I am relieved after seeing those comments targeted at you.
Huhanweibo	Let love and peace occupy the White House!
OVO	Why can't you just pay the bloody UN membership fee?
Binbin	Why don't you tweet Confucius Institute's close down in America?

3.7   CONCLUDING REMARKS

Weibo has been used actively by a number of foreign embassies. It is evident that Weibo can be employed effectively in engaging with citizens, which is one of the goals of public diplomacy. It is difficult to measure its real effects simply by looking at the data collected. In fact, one of the important phenomena this research illustrates is that, the number of followers doesn't equal to high influence, the level of "conversational" communication doesn't indicate the success of e-diplomacy. Conversely, those negative and hostile comments left on some of the embassies' Weibo accounts show that the outcome of its public diplomacy task is unsuccessful.

Future research can focus on exploring the challenges that the use of Chinese Weibo posed for foreign embassies, and to provoke thoughts about better ways to use these or other tools. It is not intended as an argument against the use of local popular social media for public diplomacy purposes, but to encourage a critical look at its practice and encourage those employing it to better analyze it.

REFERENCES

Aldama, Z. (2013, March 1). Occidente copia a China. *El país.* http://tecnologia. elpais.com/tecnologia/2013/03/01/actualidad/1362160234_435886.html.

Avery, E., Lariscy, R., Amador, E., Ickowitz, T., Primm, C., & Taylor, A. (2010). Diffusion of social media among public relations practitioners in health departments across various community population sizes. *Journal of Public Relations Research, 22*(3), 336–358.

Ayish, M. I. (2005). Virtual public relations in the United Arab Emirates: A case study of 20 UAE organizations' use of the internet. *Public Relations Review, 31*(3), 381–388.

Broom, G. M., Casey, S., & Ritchey, J. (1997). Toward a concept and theory of organization public relationships. *Journal of Public Relations Research, 9*(2), 83–98.

Business in Asia.com. (2012). The rise of China's Internet. http://www.business-in-asia.com/internet_report.html.

Chavez, M., & Hoewe, J. (2010). Reconstructing public diplomacy in the context of policy, communica on, and technology: An examination of US.–Mexico border relations. *Journal of Borderlands Studies, 25*(3⁄4), 181–190. Academic Search Complete, EBSCOhost. Accessed September 5, 2012.

ChinaLabs. (2013a, October). *The report on the effectiveness of using Internet by foreign embassies in China, Chinalabs.* http://www.huanqiu.com/attach/country/the_influence_of_websites_of_foreign_embassies_in_china_pdf.pdf. Viewed August 22, 2015.

ChinaLabs. (2013b, October). *Research report on the impact of foreign embassies'
online engagement with Chinese citizens.*http://www.huanqiu.com/attach/
country/the_influence_of_websites. Accessed August 23, 2016.

CNNIC. (2013). *The 31st statistical report on Internet development.* CNNIC.
Retrieved February 28, 2014, from http://www1.cnnic.cn/AU/SocialR/
SocialNews/201301/t20130121_38607.htm.

Cogburn, D. L., & Espinoza-Vasquez, F. M. K. (2011). From networked nomi-
nee to networked nation: Examining the impact of web 2.0 and social media
on political participation and civic engagement in the 2008 Obama campaign.
Journal of Political Marketing, 10(1/2), 191.

Curtin, P. A., & Gaither, T. K. (2004). International agenda-building in cyberspace: A study of Middle East government English-language website. *Public
Relations Review,* 30(I), 25–36.

Dashan. (2012). What is Weibo? *Quora.* Retrieved from http://www.quora.
com/What-is-Weibo.

Faina, J. (2012). Twitter and the new publicity. *ETC: A Review of General
Semantics,* 69, 55–71.

Ferguson, M. A. (1984). *Building theory in public relations: Interorganizational
relationships.* Paper presented at the meeting of the Association for Education
in Journalism and Mass Communication, Gainesville, FL.

Fisher, A. (2013, February 19). The use of social media in public diplomacy:
Scanning e-diplomacy by embassies in Washington DC. http://takefiveblog.
org/2013/02/19/the-use-of-social-media-in-public-diplomacy-scanning-e-
diplomacy-by-embassies-in-washington-dc/. Viewed August 22, 2015.

Gao, Z. (2013). China's Sina dominates Weibo by faking followers. *The Epoch
Times.* Retrieved February 28, 2014, from http://www.theepochtimes.com/
n2/china-news/chinas-sina-dominates-Weibo-by-faking-followers-351661.html.

Grant, W. J., Moon, B., & Busby Grant, J. (2010). Digital dialogue? Australian
politicians' use of the social network tool twitter. *Australian Journal of
Political Science,* 45, 579–604.

Harris, B. (2013). Diplomacy 2.0: The future of social media in nation branding. http://surface.syr.edu/cgi/viewcontent.cgi?article=1032&context=exc
hange. Viewed September 20, 2015.

Harris, V. (2014, November 24). The year the GOP stepped up its digital game, Retrieved
June 20, 2017, from https://www.harrismediallc.com/2014/11/24/vincent-harris-
gop-stepped-up-digital/.

Hayden, C. (2011). Beyond the "Obama Effect": Refining the instruments of
engagement through US. public diplomacy. *American Behavioral Scientist,* 55(6),
784–802. Academic Search Complete, EBSCOhost. Accessed September 5, 2012.

He, X., & Pedraza-Jimenez, R. (2015, March–April). Chinese social media strategies: Communication key features from a business perspective. *Profesional De
La Informacion,* 24(2), 200–209.

Hwang, S. (2011). The strategic use of twitter to manage personal public relations. *Public Relations Review,* 12, 90–92.

Kang, D. S., & Mastin, T. (2008). How cultural difference affects international tourism public relations websites: A comparative analysis using Hofstede's cultural dimensions. *Public Relations Review, 34*(1), 4–56.

Kirat, M. (2007). Promoting online media relations: Public relations departments' use of Internet in the UAE. *Public Relations Review, 33*(2), 166–174.

Leavitt, A., Burchard, E., Fisher, D., & Gilbert, S. (2009, September). The influentials: New approaches for analyzing influence on twitter. *Web Ecology Project 4.* http://www.webecologyproject.org/2009/09/analyzing-influence-on-twitter/. Accessed September 12, 2012.

Ledingham, J. A., & Bruning, S. D. (1998). Relationship management in public relations: Dimensions of an organization-public relationship. *Public Relations Review, 24*(1), 55–65.

Ledingham, J. A., & Bruning, S. D. (Eds.). (2000). A longitudinal study of organisation-public relationship dimensions: Defining the role of communication in the practice of relationship management. In *Public relations as relationship management* (pp. 55–70). Mahwah, NJ: Lawrence Erlbaum.

Levenshus, A. (2010). Online relationship management in a presidential campaign: A case study of the Obama campaign's management of its internet-integrated grassroots effort. *Journal of Public Relations Research, 22*(3), 313–335.

Lim, J. (2014). A model of functional rules for social media in the networked news sphere. *Asian Journal of Communication, 24*(3), 279–294. doi:10.1080/01292986.2013.877041.

Luo, Y. (2012). Demystifying social media use and pubic relations practice in China. In S. C. Duhe (Ed.), *New media and public relations* (2nd ed.). Bern: Peter Lang.

Marwick, A., & Boyd, D. (2011). To see and be seen: Celebrity practice on twitter. *Convergence: The Journal of Research into New Media Technologies, 17,* 139–158.

McKeown, C. A., & Plowman, K. D. (1999). Reaching publics on the web during the 1996 presidential campaign. *Journal of Public Relations Research, 11*(4), 321–347.

Men, L. R., & Tsai, W. H. S. (2012). How companies cultivate relationships with publics on social network sites: Evidence from China and the United States. In S. C. Duhe (Ed.), *New Media and Public Relations.* Bern: Peter Lang.

Mershon, P. (2012, March 28). 5 Social media tips for finding and engaging your target audience. http://www.socialmediaexaminer.com/5-social-media-tips-for-finding-and-engaging-your-target-audience-new-research/. Viewed August 22, 2015.

Ociepka, B. (2012). The impact of new technologies on international communication: The case of public diplomacy. *Information Sciences, 59,* 24–36.

Porter, J. (2009). Relationship symmetry in social networks: Why facebook will go fully asymmetric. *Bokard.* Retrieved February 28, from http://bokardo.com/archives/relationship-symmetry-on-social-networks-why-facebook-will-go-fullu-asymmetric/.

Raymond, E. (1999). The cathedral and the bazaar. *Knowledge, Technology & Policy, 12,* 23–49.

Riordan, S. (2004). Dialogue based public diplomacy: A new foreign paradigm? In D. Kelly (Ed.), *Discussion Papers in Diplomacy*. Desk top Publishing: Annette Hellinga.

Searson, E. M., & Johnson, M. A. (2010). Transparency laws and interactive public relations: An analysis of Latin American government websites. *Public Relations Review, 36*(2), 120–126.

Signitzer, B. H., & Coombs, T. (1992). Public relations and public diplomacy: Conceptual convergences. (special issue: International public relations). *Public Relations Review, 18*(2), 137–147.

Smith, B. G. (2010). Socially distributing public relations: Twitter, Haiti, and interactivity in social media. *Public Relations Review, 36*(4), 329–335.

Sullivan, J. (2014). China's Weibo: Is faster di e- rent? New media & society. *16*(1), 24–37. http://www.dx.doi.org/10.1177/1461444812472966.

Tang, K. (2014, March 3). China's netizens react to Kunming station attacks with anger, grief: Panic, calls against racial profiling, and anger at Western coverage permeate Weibo in absence of ongoing TV coverage of terror attacks. *Buzzfeed News*. http://www.buzzfeed.com/kevintang/chinese-react-to-kunming-station-attacks-with-anger#.icv3AZLn63. Viewed on August 22, 2015.

Taylor, H. (2007). The not-so-black art of public diplomacy. *World Policy Journal, 24*(4), 51–59. Academic Search Complete, EBSCOhost. Accessed September 17, 2012.

Trammell, K. D. (2006). Blog offensive: An exploratory analysis of attacks published on campaign blog posts from a political public relations perspective. *Public Relations Review, 32*(4), 402–406.

Tuch, H. N. (1990). *Communicating with the world* (p. 3). New York: St. Martins Press.

What is Public Relations? PR Definition: PRSA Official Statement. Public Relations Resources & PR Tools for Communications Professionals: Public Relations Society of America (PRSA). http://www.prsa.org/AboutPRSA/PublicRelationsDened#.UkQ1htLUkrU. Accessed September 26, 2013.

Xifra, J. (2012). New media and public diplomacy in network society-applying Manuel Castells' sociology to public society. In S. C. Duhe (Ed.), *New Media and Public Relations* (2nd ed.). Bern: Peter Lang.

Xifra, J., & Grau, F. (2010). Nanoblogging PR: The discourse on public relations in twitter. *Public Relations Review, 36*(2), 171–174.

Xu, T. (2014, April 13). Social, digital & mobile in China 2014. *We are social*. http://wearesocial.sg/blog/2014/04/social-digital-mobile-china-2014.

Yepsen, E. A. (2012). Practicing successful twitter public diplomacy: A model and a case study of US. efforts in Venezuela. *CPD Perspectives on Public Diplomacy Paper 6*.

Zaharna, R. (2010). *Battles to bridges: US. strategic communication and public diplomacy after 9/11*. New York: Palgrave Macmillan.

CHAPTER 4

Foreign Embassies' Use of Weibo

Abstract "The Use of Chinese Social Media by Foreign Embassies: Interactivity VS Influence," focuses on measuring the interactivity of those foreign embassies' Weibo accounts. It was found that awareness does not imply positive influence. Defining public diplomacy (PD) as communication with foreign publics for the purpose of achieving a foreign policy objective, PD practitioners should be cognizant that information is different than influence Wallin (The challenges of the Internet and social media in public diplomacy, American Security Project, 2013). It was also found and echoed by other researchers that the number of followers does not necessarily equate a strong connection with an audience. An account might have a million followers say nothing, even though a post gets retweeted 1000 times per day, it doesn't indicate whether those followers are supporting or against the user's communication goals.

Keywords Interactivity · Influence · Engagement

4.1 Introduction

With the rapid development of social media, a lot of corporations use it to their advantage for their brands, services, and public relations. At the same time, the public makes the most of social media for daily life including online purchasing, news reading, product information searching,

© The Author(s) 2017   69
Y. Jiang, *Social Media and e-Diplomacy in China*,
DOI 10.1057/978-1-137-59358-0_4

and for many other services and forms of entertainment. The concept 'Web 2.0' was first presented in the *O'Reilly Media Web 2.0* conference in 2004 (Graham 2005). Since then, Web 2.0 has led the evolution of social media (Kaplan and Haenlein 2010). Currently, there are various social media definitions; one of the most popular is:

> Social media is a group of Internet-based applications that build on the ideological and technological foundations of Web 2.0, and that allow the creation and exchange of user generated content. (Kaplan and Haenlein 2010)

Due to the perceived ease with which social media can be accessed and the low cost in comparison to other methods, social media platforms are seen as attractive tools for many embassies and other organizations, particularly for those are facing budget cuts and demands to increase engagement (Fisher 2013).

Social media provides the right channel to reach youth populations, which is one of the major goals of current public diplomacy efforts (Mershon 2012). For public diplomacy, it is equally important to listen to and understand young populations' thoughts, aspirations, information seeking, and other behaviors (Riordan 2004). Apart from reaching a youth audience, social media platforms also provide spaces for interaction, increased engagement, and thus furthering the goals of public diplomacy.

In addition, social media provides the opportunity to reach the youth population of other countries. Looking at foreign embassies in China, there are more than 40 embassies in China that use the most popular Chinese social media platform—Weibo to engage with Chinese citizens. Engagement and interactivity are what have been emphasized in using social media in public relation works. However, this chapter argues, interactivity doesn't necessarily link to the success of a social media account's public relation work. This chapter examines the "interactivity" of those embassies' Weibo accounts by looking at two aspects: the number of comments of retweets received by each post; the number of negative and positive comments received by each post.

According to my previous research, it is evident that Weibo can be employed effectively in engaging with citizens, which is one of the goals of public diplomacy, but it was difficult to measure its real effects simply by looking at the data collected at that stage (see Appendix). In fact, one of the important phenomena this research illustrates is that, the number of followers doesn't equal to influence, the level of "conversational" communication doesn't indicate the success of e-diplomacy. Conversely, those negative and hostile comments left on some of the embassies' Weibo accounts show that the outcomes of its public diplomacy tasks are unsuccessful.

This chapter focuses on measuring the interactivity of those foreign embassies' Weibo accounts. It was found that awareness does not imply positive influence. Defining public diplomacy (PD) as communication with foreign publics for the purpose of achieving a foreign policy objective, PD practitioners should be cognizant that information is different than influence (Wallin 2013). It was also found and echoed by other researchers that the number of followers does not necessarily equate a strong connection with an audience. An account might have a million followers say nothing, even though a post gets retweeted 1000 times per day, it doesn't indicate whether those followers are supporting or against the user's communication goals.

4.2 Literature Review

Research on the government application of new media has a long existence. In 1985, Harris, Garramone, Pizante, and Komiya were the first to discuss how computers could provide a two-way flow of information between elected officials and their constituents. McKeown and Plowman (1999) explained how 1996 US presidential candidates used the Web to reach voters during the general election, Trammell (2006) explained how blog-based attacks were utilized during the 2004 US election; Levenshus's (2010) article explained how Obama campaign utilized the Internet for grassroots efforts in Curtin and Gaither (2004). Other scholars looked at how Middle East and UAE governmental organizations used the Internet (Curtin and Gaither 2004; Ayish 2005; Kirat 2007), as well as the role of culture in country-sponsored tourism websites (Kang and Mastin 2008), the diffusion of social media in public health communication (Avery et al. 2010), and the impact of transparency laws on Latin American government websites (Searson and Johnson 2010).

Research on examining the influence of organizations' impact or influence due to the use of social media is not rare. For example, in 2013, the European Commission published a report titled "Assessing the benefits of social networks on organizations." This project aimed to analyze the current market situation for a limited number of social media stakeholders, to identify and analyze best practices for these selected stakeholders, and to define and priorities relevant policy options (European Commission 2013). This research is one of the most comprehensive pieces so far. It conducted an exhaustive and critical review of the academic, business and policy literature on the organizational use of social networking tools and social media platforms, as well as regular engagement with academic experts in this area. It was observed that while social media technologies present several potential benefits to organizations, there are considerable challenges and bottlenecks affecting adoption that may warrant policy intervention.

Apart from this relatively large-scale project on social media's influence on organizations, scholars from a range of backgrounds also examined the effectiveness of employing social media in different contexts. For example, Murthy (2015) investigated the relationship between social media and organizational collaboration, changes to organizations, and the effect of microblogging on organizations. Puijenbroek et al. (2014) focused on investigating the relationship between social media use and learning activities undertaken by employees. Kleinhans (2015) explores the potential of social media and mobile technologies to foster citizen engagement and participation in urban planning. One paper worth particular mentioning here is Nicholas Cull's article titled "The long road to public diplomacy 2.0: the Internet in U.S. public diplomacy," in this article, Cull summarized some of the successful PD examples of using new media by US government (Cull 2012). The Obama administration continued to place rhetorical emphasis on the importance of the web. Secretary Clinton spoke of protecting and advancing the digital rights of the world, by which she meant helping the citizens of Iran, China and elsewhere circumvent censorship (Cull 2012). Some posts made extensive use of new media, most famously in Indonesia, where the US embassy (after direct assistance from OIE) acquired over 200,000 additional friends on Facebook and established a digital post in a shopping mall as a new kind of Internet-age alternative to a cultural center. The embassy noted ample evidence of real dialog online and not just pleasing numbers: posts sometimes received hundreds of comments within 10 min of being posted online. There was also innovative mixing of digital media into conventional exchange projects as with OIE's "Virtual Exchange" program called (borrowing an alliterative line from President Obama's Cairo speech) "Kansas2Cairo," which introduced architecture students in Cairo to those based at the University of Southern California in Los Angeles. The students worked together in Second Life for 3 months before meeting in person for a week of direct contact, and connected far more effectively as a result.

But Cull also pointed out that not all Web 2.0 work was hailed as a success (Cull 2012, p. 17). The example used there was Coleen Graffey who had launched a personal Twitter account as a way to reveal a person behind the diplomacy and build both a positive context for US foreign policy and an audience for advocacy messages when needed (Cull 2012). As the Middle East lurched into crisis her personal tweets included details of her difficulties finding a bathing suit in Iceland to visit a spa. She was attacked for unseemly triviality (Kamen 2008) by people who failed to understand that the whole point was to present herself as a real person. At much the same time the team was pushing to launch the first formal Twitter feed for the Department and running into all sorts of objections about the inability to say anything significant in 140 characters (Cull 2012, p. 18).

However, researches on the influence of foreign embassies' in China are not that much. One of the worth mentioning publications is a report in Chinese language on Chinese foreign embassies' Internet influence published by China Labs in 2013, which analyzed the online impact level of each foreign embassy by looking at their websites and social media accounts. This report found that only 15% of foreign embassies in China opened Weibo accounts, and most of these Weibo accounts lacked interactivity. According to this report, Weibo is playing a "media" role (China Labs 2013a, b). In other words, this social media platform was used by foreign embassies as information sharing rather than influencing followers or initiating interactivity with followers. However, this research was conducted almost 4 years ago, given the rapid development of foreign embassies' use of Weibo, the research findings summarized in this report need an update.

4.3   Methods

To address the above issues, I first gathered a list of embassies on Chinese social media platforms. For the purpose of this study, the definition of an embassy's Chinese social media account refers to the embassy's official account that is verified by the service provider. It does not include any ambassador's personal account. It does not include any consular or consular staff member's account.

To gather this list, I mainly used one simple method—trawling for known embassies through Weibo's celebrity plaza (Mingren Tang), where embassies are categorized by their countries. Following this, I then gathered a list of foreign embassy Weibo users. Numerical and descriptive data (self-written Twitter biography, representative avatar, number of friends, and number of followers) were collected for each of our examined Weibo users. Further descriptive data (country and registered date) were collected and archived with both text and time/date tweeted. In order to analyze a similar series of tweets, this was then edited to a 3-month period between September 2014 and December 2014.

Based on my stage 1 research results which will be published by Routledge Handbook of Public Diplomacy in 2016 (see appendix), I selected five foreign embassies' Weibo accounts which had highest number of followers. Canada has the most followers on Sina Weibo. Canada's followers have surpassed the US and reached more than 1.1 million. US embassy has around 900,000 followers as to 6 December 2014. Cuba and the UK have same number of followers and ranked third on the list, while Korean embassy's Sina Weibo followers are slightly less than Cuba and the UK. Echoing the method of Leavitt et al. 2009), I then collected a 3-months sample of those five accounts' Weibo comments and then categorized the comments into three basic types: positive, negative, and other (irrelevant questions or ads).

4.4   FINDINGS

4.4.1   Statistics on Their Weibo Influence

The influence of each embassy on Weibo can be assessed by calculating the number of comments on their posts and the number of retweets of their posts. After analyzing the number of comments and retweets each embassy received on their Weibo from September to December in 2014, I have gathered the following results (Fig. 4.1). Korean embassy has the highest ratio of retweets and comments.

After an extremely time-consuming manual collection of comments left on these five embassies' Weibo accounts between 6 September and 6 December 2014, it is found that although US embassy has the highest level of interactivity (highest number of comments), more than half of its received comments were negative ones (Table 4.1). Although Cuba has

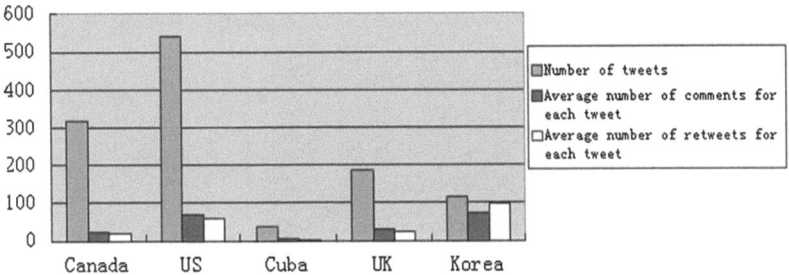

Fig. 4.1   The number of comments and retweets per post by embassies. *Source* Author's own compilation based on her own research

Table 4.1   Analysis of comments of five embassies. *Source* Author's own compilation of her research

	Canada	US	Cuba	UK	Korea
Total number of comments	7632	37,800	195	5952	8658
Positive comments	2303	5670	120	1258	6925
Negative comments	3803	22,680	0	2542	760
Other (including questions not related to the topic or ads)	1526	9450	15	2152	946

the least number of comments, most of its received comments were positives ones. Korean Embassies is also leading the way in receiving positive comments. The percentages of negative comments received by British and Canadian Embassies are just under 50% (Fig. 4.2).

4.4.2   Other Interesting Findings

Among the collected valid comments, it was evident that nationalistic sentiments toward certain Western countries are frequently presented on the embassies' Weibo accounts. According to initial statistics of 3000 negative comments received by Canadian and the US embassies, which are two embassies who have received the highest number of negative comments—most of the themes of those comments were nationalistic. For example, this is a post made by US embassy on 31 Oct 2014, it received 132 comments and most of them are negative (Figs. 4.3, 4.4). Translation:

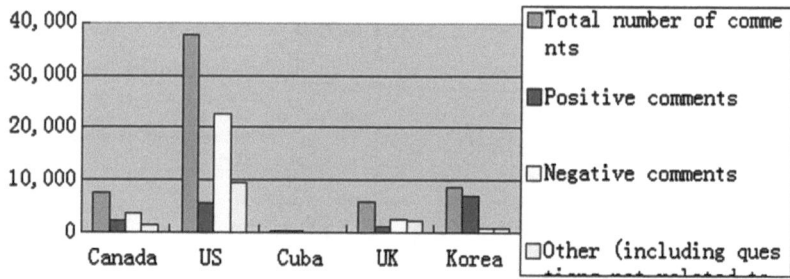

Fig. 4.2 The number of positive and negative comments received per embassy. *Source* Author's compilation based on her own research

@US Embassy in China: Around 2 million voters in America started the prior-voting process for the mid-term election on 20 Oct. President Obama has also joined them. Among the 50 states in the US, 43 of them allow pre-voting. Both parties are working hard to win the voters during this period. Due to the high competitiveness of the election, both parties are going to all lengths to win voters from every corner. What else would you like to know about mid-term election Tables 4.2, 4.3?

People might argue that the topic of this particular post was "political," and it might have attracted certain users who are in favor of China's voting system. However, even though with "non-political" topics, negative comments were apparent. For example, the following post made on the same day regarding "Halloween" by US Embassy also received ironic and hostile comments (Figs. 4.5, 4.6). Translation:

@US Embassy: Today is Halloween, it is a day deeply loved by American children although it's not an official festival, because they can wear the costumes they like, and play the "treat or trick" game. The other custom of Halloween is to decorate pumpkins. Empty a pumpkin, sculpt a face on the outside, then put a candle inside of it, the pumpkin lantern which is also called "Jack lantern" is finally completed. Does China have similar festivals?

The US embassy is not the only Western country that has received hostile comments on their posts. Nationalistic comments left on Canadian Embassy are also apparent. On 23 October 2014, a post made by Canadian Embassy says "yesterday, barbarian behavior and violent

回复@有秋意:选举团制度被创造出来时为了确保每个州都在总统选举中有代表。选举团制度迫使候选人到人口众多的地区以外展开竞选活动,照顾在直选体制下可能被忽略的地方。不赞成这种制度的人士则认为直接选举更简单明了。更多信息 网页链接

2014-10-31 15:12 来自 微博 weibo.com

Fig. 4.3 Screenshot of US Embassy's post and comments received

Fig. 4.4   Screenshot of comments left on US Embassies' posts

Table 4.2 Sample of comments received

User name	Comment
Shua Qiang	Great! People in China won't be able to see one vote in their life!
Xianshi_Taobi	Reply @wobuqirenyoutian: What's the real meaning of China's election system? We don't agree
Jiujiaowoaliaoshaba	Are you dare to give me the American visa?
Wobuqirenyoutian	China's election system is similar to most of the nations. 1200 candidates are not nominated by themselves, they are nominated by representatives from different areas, they will then be voted by people. What's wrong with this? Isn't it the same in Ukraine? Also the same in Japan, Korea? Isn't it all the same?
Wobuqirenyoutian	Those "occupiers" in Hong Kong requested a 20% threshold for election, if 20% supporting rate can represent the community, why 50% supporting rate in China's election system can't?
Djquan172	American people requests REAL election
Gangchushengjiuhensha	Fucking Americans! Why don't you sit down and talk to the people who occupied Wall Street?
Xianshitaobi	Reply @wobuqirenyoutian "Representatives need to represent the majority of people, otherwise, people will be represented without knowing who are representing them." Aren't you talking about China?
Wobuqirenyoutian	Reply @xiaoshitaobi Because I know in the circumstance of having 7 billion people in the world, the majority of us will be represented instead of representing others or ourselves. How can we have 7 billion mouths discussing one issue? Therefore, the most effective and realistic method is to elect representatives
Qingcheshuilian	America will spend estimated 4 billion US dollars on election, where does this money come from? What's the purpose of people who are providing the fund? Why spending so much on election?

terrorist attack appeared on the land of Canada, this is the second time in a week. We send our pray and memorial to the family and friends of sergeant Nathan," sergeant Nathan was died in the attack when serving in the guard of honour in Canadian national was memorial museum yesterday afternoon (translated by author from Chinese).

Table 4.3 Sample of comments received

User name	Comments
Barbie696	Why your post sounds so provoking? Of course different culture has different festivals, we don't have Halloween in China, so what?
Moxisaixiansheng	Yes we do, people who play tricks will be beaten to "Jack" face
Hongheixiaoqihao	This is a festival of Western devils, we don't need it.
Ruchunqiu	Yulanpeng festival. But it is not an entertaining day, kids will not allowed to go out after dusk
Xiaonuan-Li	We have bo lantern!
Hsia SH	We have Zhongyuan festival. It is considered a very important day by us although it's not an official festival. We use this day to commemorate our loved ones who have passed away. Do you have this type of festival in the US?
Yunjingchen	Do you have Chongyang festival to respect elderlies? Lantern's day to eat sticky rice ball? Dragon boat day to eat dragon boat? And Qingming festival to sweep the tombs of those who passed away?
Biantailadexiaohuzhu	I feel like our Spring festival is better than this festival.
Daduhuangweiwei	Feel like your post is so ironic. We have the warmth of strong family connection, do you American devils have it?
Yiyongjunjueqipingtianxia	Do you know you are retarded?
Huaren37276	So a lot of pumpkins will be wasted on this day?

However, the comments left by users are not friendly at all. Here are the translations of Table 4.4 the first 10 comments on page 1 and 2 (Figs 4.7 and 4.8):

4.5   Discussion

These results and evidence demonstrate that "conversational" communication doesn't necessarily equate to the success of e-diplomacy. Having a high number of followers and high level of interaction with your audience, does not link to positive action. Defining public diplomacy (PD) as communication with foreign publics for the purpose of achieving a

今天是万圣夜，虽然不是官方节日，却深受美国儿童的喜爱，因为这一天他们可以穿上奇 ⌄
装异服，玩"不给糖就捣乱"的游戏。万圣夜的另一个风俗是装饰南瓜。把南瓜掏空，在外
面刻出一张脸，然后在瓜中插上一支蜡烛，一个南瓜灯也叫"杰克灯"就大功告成了。请问
中国有类似的节日吗？ ✎ 网页链接

2014-10-31 10:06 来自 微博 weibo.com

收藏   转发 75   评论 104   👍56

☐ 同时转发到我的微博   评论

全部   热门   认证用户   关注的人   共104条

Barbie696：这话问的怎么这么挑衅呢。。不同的文化节日当然不一样，我们没有万圣节怎么了呀
2014-10-31 12:30   回复   👍1

默西塞先生 ★：有啊，谁捣乱直接打成杰克脸
2014-10-31 10:11   回复   👍1

红黑小7号：这是洋鬼子的节日，中国不需要
2014-10-31 10:13   回复   👍2

茹春秋 ★：盂兰盆会。但是我们一丁点没有娱乐的意思，我们就放河灯喂恶鬼烧纸钱，而且稍微懂
点儿的都不让小孩儿天黑以后出门。
2014-10-31 10:52   回复   👍2

小暖-Li ★：我们中国有波咯灯😊
2014-10-31 10:28   回复   👍1

Fig. 4.5 Screenshot of US Embassy's post and comments received

小暖-Li ★：我们中国有波咯灯😠
2014-10-31 10:28   回复 | 👍1

HsiaSh：中元节，虽然不是官方节日，但深受中国人民重视，因为这一天可以带上黄表，香纸，出
去给祖宗焚烧祭拜。中元节的另一个风俗是普渡，择日以酒肉、糖饼、水果等祭品举办祭祀活动，以
慰在人世间游玩的众家鬼魂。请问美国有类似的节日吗
2014-10-31 12:07   回复 | 👍4

云镜尘：→_→你们有重阳节孝敬老人，元宵节吃汤圆，粽子节吃粽子。清明节扫墓么？
2014-10-31 10:10   回复 | 👍2

变态辣的小户主：感觉春节全家团聚比这个更好。。。玩什么时候不是玩。。。。
2014-10-31 10:30   回复 | 👍3

公民王海滨 V 🐕：//@狗官纪事：党国只有洗脑节日！
2014-10-31 10:20   举报 | 回复 | 👍1

大肚黄维维 ★：这话的讽刺意味好浓啊!中国人过节有浓浓的亲情味，美鬼有吗？我们有中秋节如此
诗情画意的节日，你们有吗？中国春节小孩得红包，你们有吗？
2014-10-31 10:24   回复 | 👍2

以上为热门评论，查看更多»

义勇军崛起平天下：博主你脑残知道吗？
2014-11-5 19:20   回复 | 👍

华人37276：那不是要浪费很多南瓜，
2014-11-5 14:47   回复 | 👍

刚出生就很傻：操你妈了个比的美国佬，坐下来谈你妈，你怎么不和占领华尔街谈呢？操你妈了个比
的美国佬，坐下来谈你妈，你怎么不和占领华尔街比的美国佬，坐下来谈你妈，你怎么不和占领华尔
街谈呢？操你妈了个比的美国佬，坐下来谈你妈，你怎么不和占领华尔街谈呢？操你妈了个比的美国
佬，坐下来谈你
2014-11-4 02:21   回复 | 👍

现實_逃遙：回覆@大肚黄维维：其實考慮到歐洲各國文化相近，最後一句不算什麼諷刺吧...例如吧，
聖誕節英美有聖誕老人，某些國家是聖尼克，設定也不相同。對應萬聖節的簡單回答也有中元節就
好....

Fig. 4.6   Screenshot of US Embassy's post and comments received

Table 4.4   Sample of comments received

User name	Comment
Sad grassmud horse	Didn't you ask the eastern Turkish brothers in your care to say hello to Arabian?
Huang pu zhong sheng	Killed were soldiers, injured were policemen, it happened in a governmental organization's venue, attackers are now dead, there are no evidence. How can you be so sure it is a terrorist attack? If it happened in china, will western media consider it as terrorist attack or desperate action?
Warriorantigreen	You deserve it! I thought you could speak their language
Shandiren	People who are zhuangbility want to show their niubility but only reflect their shability
Zifeifanxiejiaozhilouxiajiaotang	You deserve it
Artyang77	What do you think of the terrorist attack in Xinjiang?
Sheisheibushiwo	Come on, hope you accept more Muslims, take all Muslims from China
Lan Xiao Tian	Hope Canada takes more Muslims and become a Muslim country one day
Roger is a big chubby guy	This incident only happened yesterday, it still needs investigation before determined as a "terrorist attack", the Canadian government should respect human rights of people who are involved and allow international organization to join the investigation
Ziwuyingxiao	We encourage the Canadian government to communicate with the minorities and stop suppressing the minorities

foreign policy objective, PD practitioners should be cognizant that information is different than influence. Based on the research findings, it was also arguable that the number of followers does not necessarily equate a strong connection with an audience. An account might have a million followers say nothing, even though a post gets retweeted 1000 times per day, it doesn't indicate whether those followers are supporting or against the user's communication goals.

昨天，在加拿大的国土上出现了野蛮和暴力恐怖袭击，这已经是本周第二次出现这样的事
件了。我们向下士纳森·奇里洛的家人和朋友寄予哀思及祈祷，纳森下士于昨天在加拿大国
家战争纪念馆参与礼仪仪仗队活动时遇害。

2014-10-23 14:47 来自 微博 weibo.com

收藏	转发 75	评论 106	👍 28

😊 🖼 ☐ 同时转发到我的微博			评论

全部 | 热门 | 认证用户 | 关注的人   共106条

悲伤的草泥马：你们没让收留的东突兄弟向阿拉伯人弹问好？
2014-10-26 11:24   回复 | 👍 8

皇甫钟声：被打死的是军人，受伤的是警察，袭击发生在议会大厦这个政府部门，行凶者已被击毙，
死无对证！凭什么是说是恐怖袭击？如果这事发生在中国新疆，西方媒体会怎么说？这是恐怖袭击还
是绝望的呐喊？
2014-10-24 10:49   回复 | 👍 9

Warriorantigreen：活该 你不是会飙维语吗？
2014-10-26 16:16   回复 | 👍 1

山底人：装逼被雷劈！说的就是你@加拿大大使馆官方微博
2014-10-26 16:30   回复 | 👍 1

旦嘉反邪教之楼下桥塘：活该
2014-10-26 09:48   回复 | 👍 2

artyang77：回复@皇甫钟声:对新疆暴恐攻击武警和派出所你怎么看？

Fig. 4.7   Screenshot of Canadian embassy's post and comments received

谁谁不是我：加油，希望多多收留穆斯林难民，中国的穆斯林希望你们全部接受👍
2014-10-26 17:51   回复   👍2

蓝小天：盼望加国多接纳穆斯林，早日将伊斯兰定为国教！
2014-10-26 17:32   回复   👍1

Ranger是个大胖子：这一不幸事件昨天刚刚发生，尚需深入调查，根据无罪推定原则，目前不宜简
单粗暴认定为暴力恐怖事件。请贵国充分保障事件当事人的人权，允许国际社会介入该事件的调查，
给世界人民一个满意的交代。贵国并应从深层次的体制中发现这一悲剧事件的发生原因，切实改善贵
国的人权状况，减少今后类似的悲剧。
2014-10-26 17:29   回复   👍4

轻驰紫青：我们鼓励加拿大当局与少数族裔接触，停止对少数族裔的打压
2014-10-26 17:20   回复   👍2

钟岩：这一不幸事件昨天刚刚发生，尚需深入调查，根据无罪推定原则，目前不宜简单粗暴认定为暴
力恐怖事件。请贵国充分保障事件当事人的人权，允许国际社会介入该事件的调查，给世界人民一个
满意的交代。贵国并应从深层次的体制中发现这一悲剧事件的发生原因，切实改善贵国的人权状况，
减少今后类似的悲剧。
2014-10-26 17:14   回复   👍

莫晓磊：恶之花绽放的土地 应该反思，政府为什么逼着人民造反。是不是，洋大人？
2014-10-26 17:09   回复   👍

henkelgan：坚决抗议加拿大残酷迫害MSL群众！！！加拿大政府必须反思！！
2014-10-26 17:05   回复   👍

sonicbang：咋不说是加拿大迫害穆斯林导致的正义反抗呢？继续双重标准，以后这样的事会越来越
多
2014-10-26 17:02   举报   回复   👍3

乌市汉人 ★：新疆人民给贵国发去贺电：恭喜中枪。
2014-10-26 16:59   回复   👍

四眼老丐：贵国应该尊重少数民族的合理诉求！
2014-10-26 16:31   回复   👍3

Fig. 4.8   Screenshot of Canadian embassy's post and comments received

4.6   Conclusion

Future research can look at the use of another popular social media platform in China—Wechat—by foreign embassies. Due to the different nature of Wechat, a couple of aspects might be worth comparing: (1). Are those five embassies also the most active ones on Wechat? (2). Does Wechat pose less challenges than Weibo for foreign embassies in China? This chapter is to provoke thoughts about better ways to use these social media or other tools for public diplomacy practioners. It is not intended as an argument against the use of local popular social media for public diplomacy purposes, but to encourage a critical look at its practice and encourage those employing it to better analyze it.

References

Avery, E., Lariscy, R., Amador, E., Ickowitz, T., Primm, C., & Taylor, A. (2010). Diffusion of social media among public relations practitioners in health departments across various community population sizes. *Journal of Public Relations Research, 22*(3), 336–358.

Ayish, M. I. (2005). Virtual public relations in the United Arab Emirates: A case study of 20 UAE organizations' use of the Internet. *Public Relations Review, 31*(3), 381–388.

ChinaLabs. (2013a, October). The report on the effectiveness of using Internet by foreign embassies in China, China Labs.   http://www.huanqiu.com/attach/country/the_influence_of_websites_of_foreign_embassies_in_china_pdf.pdf. Viewed on 22 August 2015.

ChinaLabs. (2013b, October). Research report on the impact of foreign embassies' online engagement with Chinese citizens. http://www.huanqiu.com/attach/country/the_influence_of_websites. Accessed 23 August 2016.

Cull, N. (2012, April 1). The long road to public diplomacy 2.0: The Internet in U.S. public diplomacy. Paper presented at the workshop "International Relationships in the Information Age," International Studies Association.

Curtin, P. A., & Gaither, T. K. (2004). International agenda-building in cyberspace: A study of Middle East government English—Language website. *Public Relations Review, 30*(1), 25–36.

European Commission. (2013). Accessing the benefits of social networks for organisations.   http://ipts.jrc.ec.europa.eu/publications/pub.cfm?id=6121. Viewed on 03 Jan 2016.

Fisher, A. (2013, February 19). The use of social media in public diplomacy: Scanning e-diplomacy by embassies in Washington DC. http://takefiveblog.org/2013/02/19/the-use-of-social-media-in-public-diplomacy-scanning-e-diplomacy-by-embassies-in-washington-dc/. Viewed on 22 August, 2015.

Graham, P. (2005, November). Web 2.0. *Paul Graham.* http://www.paulgraham.com/web20.html.

Kamen, A. (2008, December 10). In the loop: Live from Iceland, or possibly Greenland, It's the DipNote Tweet show! *Washington Post,* p. A23.

Kang, D. S., & Mastin, T. (2008). How cultural difference affects international tourism public relations websites: A comparative analysis using Hofstede's cultural dimensions. *Public Relations Review, 34*(1), 4–56.

Kaplan, Andreas M., & Haenlein, Michael. (2010). Users of the world, unite! The challenges and opportunities of social media. *Business Horizons, 53*(1), 59–68. doi:10.1016/j.bushor.2009.09.003.

Kirat, M. (2007). Promoting online media relations: Public relations departments' use of Internet in the UAE. *Public Relations Review, 33*(2), 166–174.

Kleinhans, R., Van Ham, M., Evans-Cowley, J. (2015). Using social media and mobile technologies to foster engagement and self-organization in participatory urban planning and neighbourhood governance. *Planning Practice & Research, 30*(3), 237–247.

Leavitt, A., Burchard, E., Fisher, D., & Gilbert, S. (2009, September). The influentials: New approaches for analyzing influence on twitter. *Web Ecology Project, 4.* http://www.webecologyproject.org/2009/09/analyzing-influence-on-twitter/. Accessed on 12 September 2012.

Levenshus, A. (2010). Online relationship management in a presidential campaign: A case study of the Obama campaign's management of its Internet-integrated grassroots effort. *Journal of Public Relations Research, 22*(3), 313–335.

McKeown, C. A., & Plowman, K. D. (1999). Reaching publics on the Web during the 1996 presidential campaign. *Journal of Public Relations Research, 11*(4), 321–347.

Mershon, P. (2012, March 28). 5 Social media tips for finding and engaging your target audience. http://www.socialmediaexaminer.com/5-social-media-tips-for-finding-and-engaging-your-target-audience-new-research/. Viewed on 22 August 2015.

Murthy, D. (2015, January). Introduction to the special issue on social media, collaboration, and organizations. *American Behavioral Scientist, 59*(1), 3–9.

Puijenbroek, T., Poell, R. F., Kroon, B., & Timmerman, V. (2014, April). The effect of social media use on work-related learning. *Journal of Computer Assisted Learning, 30*(2), 159–172. (14p. 1 Diagram, 9 Charts).

Riordan, S. (2004). Dialogue based public diplomacy: A new foreign paradigm? In D. Kelly (Ed.), Discussion papers in diplomacy. Desk top Publishing: Annette Hellinga.

Searson, E. M., & Johnson, M. A. (2010). Transparency laws and interactive public relations: An analysis of Latin American government Websites. *Public Relations Review, 36*(2), 120–126.

Trammell, K. D. (2006). Blog offensive: An exploratory analysis of attacks published on campaign blog posts from a political public relations perspective. *Public Relations Review, 32*(4), 402–406.

Wallin, M. (2013, February). The challenges of the Internet and social media in public diplomacy, American Security Project. https://americansecurityproject.org/ASP%20Reports/Ref%200112%20-%20Challenges%20of%20the%20Internet%20and%20Social%20Media%20in%20PD.pdf. Viewed on 12 Jan, 2016.

CHAPTER 5

A Close Case Study: Kunming Terror Attack and Embassy's e-Diplomacy via Weibo

Abstract This chapter aims to demonstrate empirically the challenges posed by Chinese cyber-nationalism in the practice of e-diplomacy on Weibo.

Keywords Cyber-mationalism · E-diplomacy · Weibo

5.1   INTRODUCTION

This Chapter is going to use American embassy's Kunming terror attack associated Weibo post on 2 March 2014 as a case study, and apply the previous explanations on why we should take a sober view on the effectiveness of using Weibo as a public diplomacy tool. By looking at this particular case study, I argue that Chinese netizens' nationalist sentiments are posing a significant challenge to foreign embassies' practice of e-diplomacy. The indicative level of "interactivity" could be misleading to some extent if contents are not looked closely.

The 2014 Kunming attack was a terrorist attack in the Chinese city of Kunming, Yunnan, on 1 March 2014. The incident, targeted against civilians, left 29 civilians and 4 perpetrators dead with more than 140 others injured. The attack has been called a "massacre" by some news media. On 2 March 2014, the US embassy made a post on its Weibo account, stated: America condemns this horrible and senseless violence

© The Author(s) 2017   89
Y. Jiang, *Social Media and e-Diplomacy in China*,
DOI 10.1057/978-1-137-59358-0_5

Table 5.1 Keywords of comments are summarized in the table below

Keywords	Frequency	Endorsed by
Orlando violence is "senseless" as well	150	3600
911 is just a traffic accident	90	5200
American imperialism	80	3000
Gun violence in America	40	2600
American should stop suppressing Muslims	30	2500

in Kunming. We send our sympathy to the families who lost their loved ones, and send our regard to everyone who is affected by this tragedy. Not long after this post, Chinese netizens expressed severe condemnation at the wording of this particular post, arguing that the use of "senseless violence" in the post demonstrates the US avoided considering this tragedy as a "terrorist attack." The US embassies' Weibo account has soon become a target for Chinese Weibo users. It received more than 50,000 comments and 30,000 retweets; most of them were focusing on interrogating the avoidance of using "terrorist attack" by US embassy in this statement. The case study of US embassy's Kunming terror attack post in this chapter aims to apply the first two expectations generated in this book: (1) Nationalistic sentiments from Chinese netizens posted on US embassy's Weibo pages pose a real challenge to Weibo diplomacy; (2) The number of comments and retweets, the level of interactivity doesn't necessarily indicate the success of e-diplomacy.

5.2   FINDINGS

5.2.1   Keywords of Comments

Softwares could automatically calculate the most frequent words used in a Chinese text were not found. Therefore, in this study, 300 comments and 300 retweets associated with this particular post were randomly picked for manual calculation (Table 5.1).

5.2.2   Key Themes of Retweets

See Table 5.2.

Table 5.2 Sample of retweets

Western / Western media bias	*e.g.* *each time there is a big incident, we see Western bias; China will remember American government's "deep friendship", stop your bias! Thanks for using your bias to teach us we should be loving our own nation*
America's double standards	e.g. American double standards disappoints me; I distrusts America because their double standards; When it comes to China, the West has double standards!

5.3 Discussion

5.3.1 The Theme of "Western Bias"

It is necessary to mention here that the anger towards the Western bias described in this chapter is not expressed by all generations in China; it is a phenomenon concentrated amongst China's Generation Y Internet users. They are proud of the accomplishments made by China, and as one journalist from Time puts it, they are "a group whose solipsistic tendencies have been further encouraged by a growing obsession with consumerism" (Elegant 2007). This particular generational focus is due to the following reason: it is this Generation Y, who embraced Western consumer culture rapidly and grew up with the Internet, and that were predicted by many Western media commentators to have the potential of posing a threat to governance of the Chinese Communist Party, and, ultimately, to be productive of more democratization.

5.3.2 Development of the Anger

Based on a series of remarkable events, I categorize the development of the anger towards Western media into five periods: year 2005, year 2006, year 2008, year 2012, and year 2016.

Year 2005: The First Stage

Chinese bloggers' complaints about the Western media started with a famous Chinese blogger Wang Jianshuo who was interviewed by the BBC in 2005. After the interview, Wang posted his unhappy feelings about the BBC on his blog:

BBC interview = censorship question interview.

There are too many predefined questions like censorship and BBC is trying to find piece of information, filter it and create an exciting picture for people in the "civilized" world (Wang 2005).

In Wang's blog, he also mentioned several other Chinese bloggers who endorsed his unhappy feelings, for example, Issac Mao and Yining, who also had experiences with Western media interviews. Yining said:

Rabiya, BBC, and all the Big Media:

Do NOT set the interviewees up, do NOT use the interviewees, do NOT manipulate them by cornering them and directing them to the opinions you yourself want to present, so to fit into your own political agenda. So if that's what you are doing, sorry, there is no way I can cooperate. Tonight, it's not about censorship, but fair and professional reporting. Censorship is another game, we will play it another day (Wang 2005).

Wang also quoted the organizer of Chinese Bloggers Conference, Issac Mao's expression of his experience with the BBC:

The reporter who called me asked whether I can speak on the LIVE program for BBC this evening London time. She was preparing the issue to be broadcast tonight at 6:45 AM London time. The topic will be the China Blogger Conference. I am pretty sure the topic will be around censorship again. I think the time is just too early for me. It is so easy to convert Greenwich Mean Time to Shanghai time, since one is GMT +0 and Shanghai is GMT +8. So I said I prefer to have a better sleep other than wake up at 4:00 AM in the morning. The other reason is, just as the previous interview, I was not 100% comfortable when I am approached with a predefined conclusion and my role is just to be an evidence to support the idea. That is neither interesting nor meaningful (Wang 2005).

Apart from Wang, an anonymous Chinese blogger also posted an article on Chinatopblog:

No surprise, BBC asked their eternal theme censorship in China. It was heard that BBC interviewed hundreds of people about this topic in their program, Yining is one of them. However Yining is a wise man, he avoided the trap. BBC commented Yining "self-censored". Oh, brother, BBC made us sick. They are more like unjust judges than reporters. I feel no wrong for what I have done (Anonymous 2005).

But these fragmentary expressions did not get the attention from the Western media till the "Great Chinese Censorship Hoax" happened in March 2006.

Year 2006: The Second Stage

On 8 March 2006, Chinese-language blogs Massage Milk and Milk Pig made the same announcements on their blog that "Due to unavoidable reasons with which everyone is familiar, this blog is temporarily closed" (Goldkorn 2006). Bloggers and journalists in the West spread the message that it was another crackdown by the Chinese government (Fowler and Qin 2006). For example, the BBC news website published that this act was a government crackdown (Usher 2006). French freepress group *Reporters Sans Frontieres* also condemned the shutdowns of the blogs in a statement (Fowler and Qin 2006). But it turned out to be a hoax; both those two blogs were back up and running after a day. Wang Xiaofeng, the author of the blog Massage Milk, expressed his intention of shutting down his blog in an interview: "to make a point about freedom of speech—just one directed at the West instead of at Beijing" (Fowler and Qin 2006, E). Wang Xiaofeng told Interfax:

I just wanted to make fun of Western journalists? [content] Doesn't need to be serious on the Internet. I don't like it that Western media take a distorted view of China, though China does have problems. I thought that if I closed my blog, it would stir their imagination and then they would begin blah blah. It really is as expected. So let they [Western journalists] have an April Fool's day in advance (MacKinnon 2006).

Later on, not only the BBC corrected its original story which indicated Chinese government's involvement in the shutdown of blogs, but also *Reporters Sans Frontieres* modified its statement on 9 March by calling the shutdown a "joke" (Fowler and Qin 2006). The Western press was commented as "irresponsible" by Wang Xiaofeng and he said that "the hoax was designed to give foreign media a lesson that Chinese affairs are not always the way you think" (ibid.). What this hoax demonstrates is Chinese bloggers' resentment of Western critics of Chinese censorship issues. And this resentment has expanded to Western negative coverage of China in 2008, and attracted the attention of the world.

Year 2008: The Third Stage

By 2008, the antipathy towards the Western media from Chinese bloggers had risen to a peak. These extreme angry sentiments were inflamed by the CNN news commentator Jack Cafferty, who described

Fig. 5.1 Photos of 2008 Tibetan Rioters (Left: Used by CNN; Right: Original Version) *Source* http://rconversation.blogs.com/rconversation/2008/03/anti-cnn-the-me.html (accessed on 20 June 2016)

Chinese products as "junk" and Chinese people as "goons" and "thugs" on CNN's political program, The Situation Room, on 9 April:

We continue to import their junk with the lead paint on them and the poisoned pet food and export, you know, jobs to places where you can pay workers a dollar a month to turn out the stuff that we're buying from WalMart. So I think our relationship with China has certainly changed. I think they're basically the same bunch of goons and thugs they've been for the last 50 years (Mostrous 2008).

After Cafferty's comments, about 6000 Chinese Americans and oversea Chinese students gathered outside CNN's studios in Los Angeles protesting his comments, demanding CNN apologize to Chinese people, and calling for Cafferty's dismissal (MacKinnon 2008).

In the middle of April 2008, YouTube videos and Facebook groups criticized CNN's coverage of the situation in Lhasa, Tibet. Chinese bloggers claimed that CNN.com had manipulated the photo of Tibetan rioters from a photograph (MacKinnon 2008). The photo used by CNN displayed a military vehicle chasing protesters (see Fig. 5.1, left); the original version showed a different scenario: Tibetan rioters appear to be attacking military vehicles (see Fig. 5.1, right). Chinese bloggers argued that CNN manipulated the photo intentionally to tell a particular story.

Together with the inflammation comments by Cafferty, this controversial photo led to a website called "anti-CNN", established by one Chinese blogger. The website states, "We are not against the Western media, but against the lies and fabricated stories in the media. We are not against the Western people, but against the prejudice from the Western society" (www.anti-cnn.com/index5.html). The website claims that the Western media's "misidentifications are intentional, part of an agenda on the part of the Western media" (Zuckerman 2008). As Kennedy from Global Voices translates:

> For a long time now, certain western media best represented by CNN and BBC, in the name of press freedom have been unscrupulously slandering and defaming developing nations. In order to achieve their unspoken goal, they mislead and they ensnare, switching black for white, confusing right and wrong, fabricating...willing to go to any length [Original texts posted on http://www.anti-cnn.com/index2.html in Chinese] (Translation by John Kennedy on Global Voices Online, 24 March 2008).

The anger towards the Western media then became widespread in Chinese cyberspace and raised to an extremely high degree amongst Chinese bloggers. The comments on the anti-CNN forum posted by average Chinese have overwhelmingly expressed anger over the "Western media biased" coverage, and their anger has become even more intensified. The website "Anti-CNN" is currently still continuously supplying textual, photographic, audio, and video examples display North American and European media's allegedly misrepresentations the situation in stories about China. As Chinese bloggers indicate, it will be a "long-term battle":

This is a struggle of resistance against western hegemonic discourse. We need to fully recognize that this will be a long-term, difficult and complex battle. But regardless of the outcome, we all firmly believe: Western nations' days of using several of their crap media in an absurd attempt to fool people with their rotten words will soon be over for good! [Original texts posted on http://www.anti-cnn.com/index2.html in Chinese] (Translation by John Kennedy on *Global Voices* 24th March 2008).

Year 2012: The Fourth Stage

China's Ye Shiwen won gold in the women's 400-m individual medley at 2012 London Olympics, breaking the world record by a second. She swam her final 50-m freestyle in 28.93 s, which was faster than the American winner of the men's event Ryan Lochte's final 50 m (29.1 s). This prompted John Leonard, an American who is the executive director of the World Swimming Coaches Association, to call Ye's gold-medal performance "suspicious" in an interview with the Guardian.

Western media started questioning Ye's performance, for example, Rick Morrissey from Chicago Sun-time wrote: "For those who believe a person is innocent until proven guilty, good for you. But for we skeptics, the people who have seen athletes try to beat the system over and over again, it's impossible to look at Ye's performance Monday and not suspect that something is very, very wrong" (Morrissey 2012). BBC's sport commentator Clair Bauldin even expressed her concern to the whole world at the scene.

The allegation has set off a furious response in China, where the Olympics are closely followed. China took the most gold medals at the Beijing Games in 2008, a point of national pride and a sign of the country's resurgent national strength. The head of China's Olympic swimming team rejected any suggestion that Ye may have used performance-enhancing drugs.

On 30 July, the alleged BBC's biased suspicion first criticized by Chinese netizens on Sina Weibo, and started gathering attention from netizens. By 31 July, it was reposted for more than 20,000 times on Sina Weibo, and on the next day, Chinese state media broadcast the story and questioned the Western media bias in the suspicion of Ye Shiwen doping.

On 6 August, a prestigious academic journal *Nature* apologized to Chinese swimmer. Ye Shiwen for carrying a controversial article on its website that "gave the impression that we were supporting accusations against her" with implication for doping.

Year 2016: The Fifth Stage

In June 2016, a new song called "This is China" aiming to tell Westerners the "truth" about China was released by a group of young Chinese rappers. It has been making international headlines after it was posted by the Chinese Communist Youth League on their Weibo account. The video features Chengdu rap group CD REV spitting lines such as "China is a developing country/It has a large population and is really hard to manage in an attempt to correct what they see as misleading portrayals of the country in Western media" (Beech 2016).

The rap has received mostly positive feedback on Weibo, with comments ranging from users saying how much they loved the country, to others saying they had been reduced to tears. "Although we have many shortcomings, little by little, we can make our country stronger and our lives better," said one such comment (BBC 2016).

The fifth stage nationalism wave has also been highlighted in the 2016 Rio Olympic Games. Australian TV station Channel Seven outraged members of the Chinese community in Sydney by broadcasting a photo of the Chilean flag instead of the Chinese flag during a segment which predicted the top five medalists at the 2016 Rio Games. The 2016 Rio Olympics didn't just mark the ascendance of major Chinese athletes like swimmer and Internet darling Fu Yuanhui—it also demonstrated how Chinese nationalism can affect the global online dialog (Ruan 2016). During the games, Australian gold medalist swimmer Mack Horton called Chinese competitor Sun Yang a "drug cheat"; in response, Chinese netizens flooded Horton's accounts on Facebook, Twitter, and Instagram—all of which are blocked in China and can only be accessed with censorship circumvention tools—to demand an apology.

But members of this latest group jumping over China's so-called great firewall of censorship don't necessarily fit the well-worn trope of the young, angry male Internet troll. On what seems to be Horton's personal account on Chinese social media site Weibo, for example, Chinese users left over 243,000 recent comments under a 2015 post, most calling Horton a "loser." A Weibo analytics tool developed by prestigious Peking University shows 83% of these users identifying as female. Some were likely part of an increasingly high-profile, active, and young female-dominated online group commonly called the "Little Pink" (Ruan 2016).

5.4   The West's Double Standards

On 18 November, the French magazine Le Nouvel Observateur (The New Observer) published an article on its website authored by staff writer Ursula Gauthier, which blamed the Chinese government's policies in the Xinjiang Uygur autonomous region for terrorist attacks in China. That was seen as a typical example of the West's double standard by Chinese (China Daily 2015). The article published by China Daily on 23 November 2015 stated "being politically radical has so blinded some Western journalists such as Gauthier that they lose their common sense" (China Daily 2015). It argued that Western media only know Western standards of "human rights." For that political purpose they dare to challenge the basic human norm that the killing of innocent civilians is a crime.

The posts left on US embassy's Weibo post regarding Kunming terror attack endorse the argument in the above paragraph. Many comments and retweets criticized the double standard approach that the US employs in defining "terrorist attacks." One of the most frequent mentioned sentences in the comments is "If you define '301 Kunming terrorist attack' as 'horrible and senseless violence', '911' would then be an 'unluckily traffic accident!'"

There is truth in China's accusation that the West holds a double standard when it comes to classifying acts of extremist violence within China as acts of terrorism (Liu 2016). The Western narrative depicts such attacks as the result of China's own flawed ethnic-minority policies and religious crackdown on Uighur Muslims who mostly live in the Northwestern Xinjiang Autonomous Region (Liu 2016). As such, violent attacks in China, mostly conducted by Uighur extremists, appear to be somewhat different from attacks conducted by Al-Qaeda or ISIS elsewhere. For instance, in the aftermath of the shocking Kunming train station attack in March 2014 that left 31 people dead and another 141 injured, the *BBC* called the event a "deadly mass knife attack" and quoted "Uighur activists" as worrying that the attack could open up "potential for abuse" by the Chinese state (BBC 2014). Little wonder the veiled suggestion that the attack had some legitimate political motives and the portrayal of the attackers as victims of oppression angered Chinese citizens, who in turn accused Western media of hypocrisy in its labeling of terror (Xinhua 2014).

As Liu points out, while admittedly much can be improved in China's minority policies and in its treatment of religious, especially Islamic, activities, there should be no hesitation to view such attacks in China as acts of terrorism (Liu 2016). Though these attacks may be caused to a greater extent by the economic dislocation of the Uighur on China's frontiers than the direct recruitment and command of Al-Qaeda or ISIS, one must ask: how is a radicalized Muslim minority in China fundamentally different than such groups in the Middle East or South Asia that have similarly lost prospect of economic advancement and regard militant Islamic fundamentalism as the only recourse? Liu also argues that Western media needs to acknowledge that Islamic networks overseas do pose a security threat to China (Liu 2016). The East Turkestan Islamic Movement (ETIM), a US-designated terrorist organization that calls for the separation of Xinjiang to become part of an independent Islamic state, has a broad support base in Central Asia and Turkey, as indicated by an anti-China riot in Istanbul in 2015 (Reuters 2015). If knife-wielding attackers at a train station calling for the separation of China do not qualify as terrorists, then perhaps the definition of "terrorism" should be expanded.

However, Liu also advocates that at the same time, it is necessary for China to reject its own double standard regarding terrorism in order to fully tackle the issue. While the Chinese government has frequently stated its opposition to any and all forms of terrorism, a popular myth continues to exist in China that considers terrorism solely as the product of the West's own wrongdoing (Hewitt 2015). The prevalent anti-Western Chinese nationalism supported by the state has led many Chinese citizens to develop sympathies for Islamic terrorist organizations, which claim that the Muslim world's suffering has come at the hands of the US. As a result, a considerable minority in China perceives groups like Al-Qaeda as anti-American heroes and even cheered for them after 9/11 (Zhou 2001). For those who hold a less sanguine view of these groups, they nonetheless blame the West for having fostered the growth of groups like Al-Qaeda as proxies against the Soviet Union. What they fail to acknowledge is the fact that China, too, provided military assistance to the Mujahideen during the Soviet invasion of Afghanistan (Hilali 2001). Furthermore, the lack of high-profile terrorist attacks in China has augmented the belief that the problem of terrorism afflicts only the West, and that China can remain safely on the sideline.

China's criticism on the US double standards has actually been a regular theme in international news. For example, in Febuary 2016, China criticized the US of "double standards" on South China Sea row (The Hindu 2016). In November 2016, China's government responded to the Paris terror attacks and criticized the west for "double standards" (Anderlini and Shepherd 2016). In May 2015, Chinese envoy accused the US of double standards over South China Sea disputes (Chan 2015) In December 2014, China accused the US of human rights "double-standards" (Phillips 2014). Those are just a few examples from the searched results. It is apparent that Chinese strongly believes that the US and the West in general employ double standards when it comes to China-related issues, which was clearly endorsed in the comments and retweets left on the US embassy's Weibo account in the case study in this Chapter. Therefore, Weibo as an e-diplomacy tool is very limited in terms of improving the West's public image in China. It is arguable that these efforts on promoting two-way communication and increasing the level of interactivity are not helping the key aims of the embassies.

5.5   Conclusion

The case study of US embassy's Kunming terror attack post in this chapter illustrated two expectations generated in this book: (1) Nationalistic sentiments from Chinese netizens posted on US embassy's Weibo pages pose a real challenge to Weibo diplomacy. Those large amount of negative comments have a great impact on US embassy's public image. (2) The number of comments and retweets, the level of interactivity doesn't necessarily indicate the success of e-diplomacy. In this particular case, looking at a superficial level, the original Weibo post received good level of responses from the target audience.

References

Anderlini, J. & Shepherd, C. (2016, November 30). China rebukes west for terror "double standards". *Financial Times*. Retrieved September 12, 2016, from http://www.ft.com/cms/s/0/8a5463e4-8d14-11e5-a549-b89a1dfede9b.html#axzz4JjO7SJoE.

Anonymous. (2005). 10 August, viewed 23 April 2017.

BBC. (2014, September 12). Four sentenced in China over Kunming station attack. *BBC News*. Retrieved October 10, 2016, from http://www.bbc.com/news/world-asia-china-29170238.

BBC. (2016, June 30). Party propaganda rap aims to "tell foreigners truth" about China. *BBC News*. Retrieved September 12, 2016, from http://www.bbc.com/news/world-asia-china-36670095.

Beech, H. (2016, 30 June). This Chinese propaganda rap is the most painful song ever recorded. *The Times*. http://time.com/4388991/china-rap-propaganda-cd-rev/. Viewed on 12 September 2016.

Chan, M. (2015, May 15). "Just who is creating tensions?" Chinese envoy accuses US of double standards over South China Sea disputes. *South China Morning Post*. Retrieved September 12, 2016, from http://www.scmp.com/news/article/1797501/us-blame-tension-south-china-sea-says-beijing.

China Daily. (2015, November 23). Double standard on terrorism is symptomatic of West's view. Retrieved September 12, 2016, from http://www.chinadaily.com.cn/opinion/2015-11/23/content_22509850.htm.

Elegant, S. (2007, July 26). China's Me Generation. *The Times*. Retrieved August 26, 2016, from http://www.time.com/time/magazine/article/0,9171,1647228-1,00.html.

Fowler, G. A. & Qin, J. (2006, March 14). Chinese bloggers stage hoax. *Wall Street Journal*. p. B3.

Goldkorn, J. (2006, 27 April). Danwei TV 7: Muzi Mei sex blogger. http://www.danwei.org/danwei_tv/danwei_tv_7_mu_zimei_interview.php. Viewed 23 April 2016.

Hewitt, D. (2015, November 16). China to step up counterterrorism measures after Paris attacks, calls for international support against Xinjiang Separatists. *International Business Times.* Retrieved September 18, 2016, from http://www.ibtimes.com/china-step-counterterrorism-measures-after-paris-attacks-calls-international-support-2185525.

Hilali, A. Z. (2001). China's response to the Soviet Invasion of Afghanistan. *Central Asian Survey, 20*(3), 323–351. doi:10.1080/02634930120095349.

Liu, Z. (2016, February 16). China and the West: Time to end double standards on terrorism. *Diplomacist.* Retrieved October 11, 2015, from https://diplomacist.com/2016/02/19/china-and-the-west-time-to-end-double-standards-on-terrorism/.

Mackinnon, R. (2006, March 14). The great Chinese censorship hoax. *Rconversation.* Retrieved February 25, 2017, from http://rconversation.blogs.com/rconversation/2006/03/the_great_chine.html.

Mackinnon, R. (2008, March 26). Anti-CNN and the Tibet information war. *Rconversation.* Retrieved February 25, 2016, from http://rconversation.blogs.com/rconversation/2008/03/anti-cnn-the-me.html.

Morrissey, R. (2012, July 31). China's Ye Shiwen raises doping suspicion with 'impossible' win. *Chicago Sun- time.* Retrieved August 12, 2016, from http://www.suntimes.com/sports/olympics/14121090-777/story.html.

Mostrous, A. (2008, April 16). CNN Apologizes to China Over "thugs and goons" comment by Jack Cafferty. *Times Online.* Retrieved April 23, 2016, from http://www.timesonline.co.uk/tol/news/world/article3756437.ece.

Phillips, T. (2014, December 9). China accuses US of human rights "double-standards". *The Telegraph.* Retrieved September 12, 2016, from http://www.telegraph.co.uk/news/worldnews/asia/china/11282190/China-accuses-US-of-human-rights-double-standards.html.

Reuters. (2015, July 5). China says tourists attacked in Turkey during anti-China protests. *Reuters.* Retrieved July 12, 2016, from http://www.reuters.com/article/us-china-turkey-idUSKCN0PF08L20150705.

Ruan, L. (2016, August 25). The new face of Chinese nationalism. *Foreign Policy.* Retrieved September 12, 2016, from http://foreignpolicy.com/2016/08/25/the-new-face-of-chinese-nationalism/.

The Hindu. (2016, February 21). China accuses U.S. of "double standards" on South China Sea row. *The Hindu.* Retrieved September 12, 2016, from http://www.thehindu.com/news/international/china-accuses-us-of-double-standards-on-south-china-sea-row/article8264407.ece.

Usher, S. (2006, March 8). China shuts down outspoken blog. *BBC News*. Retrieved October 20, 2016, from http://news.bbc.co.uk/2/hi/asia-pacific/4787302.stm.

Wang, J. S. (2005, November 7). BBC's Interview. *Wangjianshuo's Blog*. Retrieved April 26, 2016, from http://home.wangjianshuo.com/archives/20051107_bbcs_interview.htm.

Xinhua. (2014, March 3). Distorted Western coverage of Kunming terror attack reveals shameful double standard. Retrieved September 09, 2016, from http://www.globaltimes.cn/content/845815.shtml.

Zhou, Z. C. (2001). After 911 terror attack, 6th October 2015. *Modern Chinese Studies*. Retrieved November 03, 2016, from http://www.modernchinastudies.org/us/issues/past-issues/75-mcs-2001-issue-4/596-911.html.

Zuckerman, E. (2008, March 25). Bridgeblogging Chinese anger over perceived media bias. Retrieved July 23, 2016, from http://www.ethanzuckerman.com/blog/2008/03/25/bridgeblogging-chinese-anger-over-perceived-media-bias/.

PART III

Public Diplomacy and Weibo

CHAPTER 6

Weibo as a Public Diplomacy Platform

Abstract "Weibo as a public diplomacy tool", borrows the "three-dimension framework" from Bjola and Jiang (in: Bjola and Holmes (eds) Digital diplomacy: theory and practice, Routledge, New York, 2015), discusses each dimension in relation to the empirical data in previous chapters.

Keywords Two-way communication · Weibo · Public diplomacy tool

6.1 INTRODUCTION

The application of social media to the field of diplomacy has been hailed as a transformative development of international politics (Stein 2011; Seib 2012). Not only is social media able to transcend hierarchical chains of diplomatic communication, but by bringing ordinary people into the spotlight of political life and making their voice heard, it also allows diplomats to directly engage foreign publics in a sustained dialog (Bjola and Jiang 2015, p. 71). These critical changes and their consequences largely explain why social media has become such a powerful symbol of the "new public diplomacy". Diplomats now have the possibility not only to promote a message unidirectionally, but also to carry on enlightening conversations with a broad segment of the population of the country in which they operate (ibid. p. 71). On the other hand, scholars point out that there is the discrepancy between the belief in public relations

© The Author(s) 2017   105
Y. Jiang, *Social Media and e-Diplomacy in China*,
DOI 10.1057/978-1-137-59358-0_6

and public diplomacy research and practice that the use of social media will lead to more two-way communication (Renken 2014). This discrepancy manifests for instance in government agencies and diplomatic missions trying to engage in modern dialogic online communication with what they assume are the correct or interested publics for their messages, while still being stuck in old top-down structures of information delivery (Renken 2014). This results not only in communication efforts that are less effective than they could be, but also shows the challenges and risks to the use of social media for public diplomacy efforts, like a loss of control over content and the challenge to use informal platforms for the communication of missions that are used to formal communication (Renken 2014).

To effectively examine Weibo as a public diplomacy tool, this chapter will review public diplomacy tools historically, then examine social media as public diplomacy tools generally, followed by borrowing the "three-dimensions framework" from Bjola and Jiang (2015), to discuss each dimension in relation to the empirical data in previous chapters.

6.2   REVOLUTION OF PUBLIC DIPLOMACY TOOLS

In November 1967, President Lyndon Johnson's public diplomacy star, Leonard Marks, who as director of the US Information Agency (USIA) oversaw US engagement with public opinion around the world, spoke to the National Association of Educational Broadcasters (Cull 2012). He presented "a Blueprint for a New Schoolhouse". A vision of what he called "a worldwide information grid" lay at its core. Educators, he argued, needed not only to "collect knowledge electronically" but also "learn how to route it sensibly... or it will surely rout us". This had ethical implications: "we must learn to share our knowledge with our neighbors so that all may benefit". Marks imagined this *worldwide grid* linking Cambridge, Massachusetts with Cambridge, England; Moscow, Idaho and Moscow, U.S.S.R.; and centers of learning across the developing world: "a unique method of plugging together human minds between any points on earth". Marks highlighted the coming revolution of electronic data exchange: "A system of electronic interchange of information could readily be set up within the next 5 years—provided we make imaginative use of the satellites, and link them to information storage and retrieval systems already in existence" (Marks 1967). Marks returned to this theme in a further speech in February 1968: a world information grid of linked computers would, he argued, be "a fundamental step toward lasting world peace..". (Marks 1968).

Forty years later, individuals are able to connect internationally using small devices that can be fit in a pocket (Cull 2012). More than this, Marks imagined complete messages and datasets being transferred rather than an electronic architecture capable of allowing individuals to collaborate and generate their own content. But technology was only a means to an end imagined by Marks (Cull 2012). His vision was one of peace built from equitable exchange between minds around the world not the digital hegemony of one preeminent actor. Not all the advocates of US public diplomacy—digital or otherwise—have shared Marks's vision. The debates that have characterized public diplomacy in the analog era have continued in the digital.

The term public diplomacy—the conduct of foreign policy by engagement with a foreign public—is relatively new, acquiring this meaning only in 1965 (Cull 2012). The activity is, in contrast, as old as statecraft. As Cull has argued in his 2009 work, the principle areas of public diplomacy work have been: listening (engaging a foreign public by listening to it and channeling what is learned into policy formation); advocacy (engaging a foreign public by explaining ones policies and/or point of view); cultural diplomacy (engaging a foreign public by facilitating the export of one's culture such as arts or language); exchange diplomacy (engaging a foreign public by facilitating direct contact between one's own people and a foreign population); and international broadcasting (engaging a foreign public through the provision of news according to the accepted mores of international journalism) (Cull 2009).

Although like Web 2.0 the term Public Diplomacy 2.0 has never been used with particular precision, three key characteristics emerge: The first characteristic is the capacity of the technology to facilitate the creation of relationships around social networks and online communities. The second characteristic is the related dependence of Public Diplomacy 2.0 on user-generated content from feedback and blog comments to complex user-generated items such as videos or mash-ups. The third characteristic is the underlying sense of the technology as being fundamentally about horizontally arranged networks of exchange rather than the vertically arrange networks of distribution down which information cascaded in the 1.0 era (Cull 2012). While the technology is entirely new the underlying pattern of relationships underlying the operation of Public Diplomacy 2.0 is not.

During the past decade, public diplomacy research has received much attention from communication scholars. Unlike traditional diplomacy that focuses on nation-to-nation relationships, public diplomacy examines the relationships between governments (Gilboa 2000; Manheim 1994), nongovernmental organizations (Zhang and Swarts 2009), and corporations (Molleda 2011) and citizens of other nations. As explained by Wang (2006), nations use public diplomacy tactics to promote their desired image and build relationships with nations and their people. Inspired by Nye's (2005, 2008) soft power approach, several public diplomacy studies have examined international cooperation programs, including cultural diplomacy and educational exchanges (Schneider 2003; Snow 2008), aid diplomacy (Lancaster 2007), health diplomacy (Wise 2009), sports diplomacy (Xifra 2009), and even water diplomacy (Karaev 2005).

Recognizing the complex interaction between government programs, global news coverage, and international public opinion, scholars have argued for the examination of public diplomacy through a public relations perspective (Fitzpatrick 2007; L'Etang 2009; Signitzer and Coombs 1992). Signitzer and Wasmer (2006) have asserted that public diplomacy is a specific governmental function of public relations whose goals are intertwined. Ultimately, public diplomacy is focused on the establishment and maintenance of a mutual beneficial relationship between governments and foreign citizens (Gilboa 2008; Signitzer and Coombs 1992; Yun 2006). This goal is consistent with the body of public relations literature that focuses on relationship management (Grunig and Huang 2000; Ki and Hon 2007; Ledingham 2003) and stewardship (Hon and Grunig 1999; Waters 2009, 2011). Because of this focus on relationships, many scholars have asserted that the public relations perspective provides a relevant construct for scholarship on public diplomacy (L'Etang 1998, 2008; Signitzer and Wasmer 2006; Wang 2006).

6.3   Illustrating Example

The study on the German missions' Facebook use by Renken (2014) is an excellent example here to endorse the findings of Weibo as a public diplomacy tool. Renken identifies that there is a discrepancy between the expectations towards social media and what they can realistically deliver. In order to find out whether the social media communication of the German missions is as symmetrical, two-way, and dialog based as the FFO wants it to be according to its own mission statement, a first content analysis of the mission's Facebook profiles was conducted. Renken had two research questions:

RQ1:   What strategy is primarily used according to van Ruler's communication grid? Are the missions engaging in dialog online as they and the ministry claim to do?

        After determining the current status of the social media communication, Renken's study attempts to answer the following research question and sub-questions in order to explain the present situation, using in-depth content analysis and a survey distributed to the missions.

RQ2:   What role does the social media presence of the missions play in the public diplomacy efforts of the FFO?

SQ1:   What are the concrete expectations and goals the FFO and the missions place on their social media presence?

SQ2:   What are the challenges of the use of social media in public diplomacy?

Renken found that the 32 missions published a total of 111 Facebook posts within the period of analysis. The posts were not distributed equally between the missions; five missions did not publish any posts during the period (Bangalore, Edinburgh, Jeddah, Karachi, and Pretoria), while the highest number of posts was published by the mission in New Delhi (10 posts in total). The survey was completed by 15 German missions abroad. Additionally, nine missions informed the researcher that they could or would not participate. Several missions asked to receive the questionnaire via official FFO channels because they did not feel comfortable answering it coming from an unknown source (e.g. Chisinau). These requests as well as the low response rate prove Fowler's point "when survey requests come from less known or unknown sources […] sometimes, virtually no one responds" (2009, p. 103). The researcher contacted several appropriate departments within the FFO but these efforts were not met with success. According to Annette Walz, who works in the department for the Training of International Diplomats in the FFO, every electronic document that is sent out via an FFO email address has to be approved internally first. In a personal conversation on 8 April 2014, she said that there is a certain "paranoia when it comes to sending out documents that are not originating from within the FFO" (Walz 2014). This proves Hocking's point that while public diplomacy is adapting to pressures for change, there still tend to be a lot of "top-down processes" with the foreign ministries and the diplomatic services taking the function of "gatekeepers" (2005, p. 36).

According to the survey results in Renken's study, the main expectation towards social media use in public diplomacy perceived by the missions is the ability to have a dialog with their publics. In fact, when asked why they are using Facebook, the answer from each mission included a reference to dialog. For instance, Stockholm wants to "establish and maintain communication with the public". All missions have the comment function enabled, meaning users can comment on the posts the mission published. The missions see this as a possibility to start a dialog or a discussion with users and to receive feedback for their work. The mission in Sofia explains that in Bulgaria the threshold of getting in touch with state institutions is generally quite high and that they want to make a difference. They "do not want to project the image of being 'unapproachable'". The mission in Windhoek gives the textbook answer: "two-way communication is important in social media". However, the missions have made the experience that dialog does not happen simply because the possibility is there (Kent and Taylor 1998, p. 324). For instance, the mission in Dhaka reports "we want to engage in discussions with users but it [the comment function] is not frequently used by users" (2014). Dialog is not seen as only positive however, the missions are aware of dangers and difficulties connected to public dialog online. As the mission in Brussels reflects: "the advantage of being able to have a dialogue with the public can sometimes turn into a disadvantage when the response is questionable or in bad taste".

The second expectation identified is an increased reach for the mission's messages. The main target groups of the missions are the public of the host country and Germans living or traveling in the host country. Within those two groups, the audience is mostly young and urban. One of the main functions of Facebook is advertising the events that the missions or partners of the FFO (like for instance the Goethe Institute) organize. Since the FFO emphasizes the orientation towards audiences by tailoring projects and offers to specific audiences, a lot of the events are focused on education and scholarships, thereby targeting potential students and educated young people specifically. The use of Facebook gives the missions access to young people who are interested in education offers and who would not be reached through more traditional media. "We reach a younger public that would otherwise not be interested in the embassy's work" (Warsaw 2014). Connecting with the young people through education and thus developing networks is one of the major pillars of the FFO's public diplomacy strategy.

In the analysis of the posts and well as in the results of the survey, three communication goals could be identified: *informing*, *advertising*, and *attempting to start a dialog.*

Supporting the finding of the first content analysis, most posts could be categorized as *informing* the visitors. The missions are mainly informing about German culture and research and education but also about current news for instance in politics. This is very much in line with the FFO's aim of strengthening of Germany as a base for education and scientific activities as well as creating a positive and modern image of Germany and attaining sympathy abroad (Auswärtiges Amt 2013, p. 7). The mission in Canberra for instance tries to show that "Germans are not dead serious" by having a lot of funny posts about German traditions and giving insights into the mission by regularly posting "behind the scenes" information like baking and cooking recipes collected from the staff. Posts about the host country are concentrated on reports and pictures from past events, administrative issues (such as job postings) as well as the host country's culture and current news. However, some missions also try to shape the public opinion about issues in their host country that will not be discussed in the local mainstream media; "We use social media to boost key issues like human rights, that will not be picked up by the local media in Vietnam" (Hanoi 2014). This illustrates that online public diplomacy is not only used to develop an understanding and respect for the German culture, but also to promote values like freedom and human rights (Auswärtiges Amt 2013, p. 7).

The second largest amount of posts was connected to the *advertising* of events organized by the missions or by their partners like Goethe Institute or the German Information Centers. Here the missions are implementing two further aims of the FFO, namely the promotion of the German language abroad through public—private partnerships, like the close cooperation with the Goethe Institute, and the creation of a cultural exchange and presentation of German art and culture abroad (Auswärtiges Amt 2013, p. 7). The mission in Sofia reports: "We use Facebook to advertise our events, e.g. the "Bildungsbörse" (education fair). Facebook gives us access to a specific target group, young people who are interested in German education offers.

Both, the FFO and the missions, state clearly that they expect to engage in a dialog with their audience through the use of social media. The missions value that their Facebook profiles are accessible for many people who would not have the opportunity to visit the mission or their events physically, and that Facebook is easy to use and requires little training for the employees. Also, social media are seen as a cost-effective way to disseminate information. Furthermore, missions clearly understand dialogic potential of social media like the possibility for two-way communication, receiving feedback, and the possibility to answer fast to questions but they are not able to implement this knowledge into dialog. Many missions wish they were able to engage in more dialog (e.g. Istanbul, Mexico City, and Stockholm 2014). The following section will look at Weibo from the "three-dimensions" before looking at the challenges and problems of using it as a public diplomacy tool.

6.4   The Three-Dimensions

6.4.1   Agenda-Setting

To understand how foreign embassies used Weibo as an agenda-setting platform, I selected Korean embassy and US embassy as two samples, and categorized all posts sent during the selected timeframe based on the original topic of discussion (see Figs. 6.1 6.2). In the case of Korean embassy, posts are categorized into seven groups: China–Korea cooperation, Korea news, Korea society, Korea tradition, offline activity, language, and travel. In the case of US embassy, posts are categorized into China–US cooperation, US news, US culture, US history, offline activity, Visa, travel, and US state.

A close look at the two Weibo accounts reveals important patterns and regularities. First, the frequency of daily posts, all written in Chinese, is surprisingly stable. The number of embassy posts totaled 306 and 478 for Korea embassy and US embassy, respectively, and those posts were evenly spread throughout the 50-day period. Clearly, posting on Weibo has become a regular activity for the delegation and the embassies, which suggests that dedicated staff must be in charge of carrying out this task. Second, the design of Weibo feeds shows a crafty combination of informative texts, lively pictures, and hyperlinks to policy papers. A balance is actually struck between the effort to stimulate the interest of Weibo users in an entertaining manner and the need to maintain an authoritative

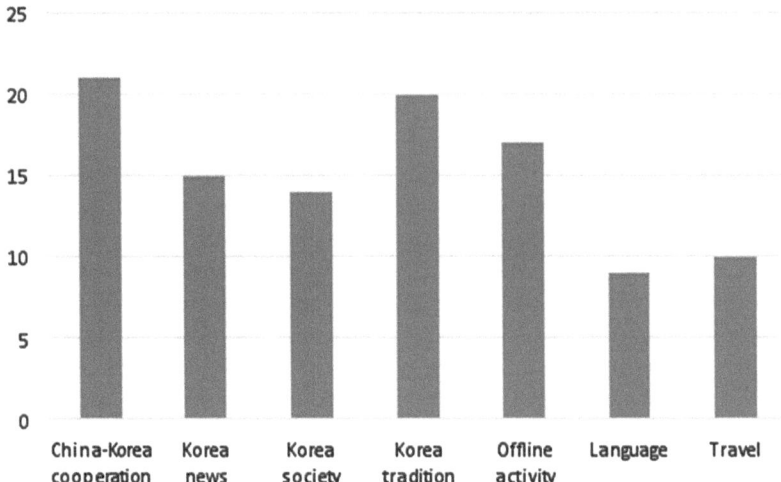

Fig. 6.1   Weibo entries of the Korean embassy

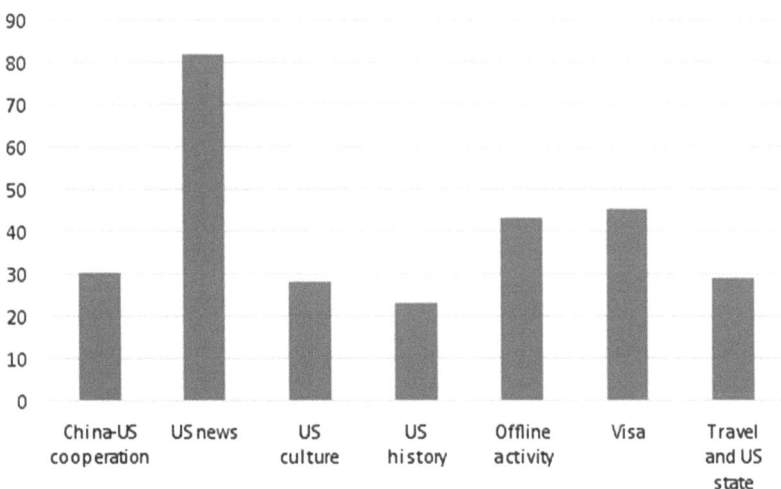

Fig. 6.2   Weibo entries of the US embassy

stance and provide official messages. Third, each Weibo account follows a specific content pattern. For example, the US embassy offers daily or weekly information on fixed topics. But the focus of each account is slightly different, a fact that reflects the different agenda-setting strategies and styles pursued by each embassy.

For instance, Korean embassy exerts a strict control over its agenda, as suggested by the topics it chooses to post about but equally important by those it chooses not to post on Weibo. First, there is an explicit and active classification of posts according to their content. Each post falls into one of about 10 topics (Korean cuisine, Korea news, Korea—China cooperation, Korean society, Korean tradition, activities, language learning etc.), the name of which is usually highlighted in square brackets before each post. In this way, the embassy actually frames the topic in the way it wants the audience to understand. Second, there is a strong focus on nonpolitical topics. As can be seen from these posts, the Korean account provides information on a wide range of topics such as food, travelling, and traditions, while there are hardly any posts on trade, economy, or other politically related topics. Of all Korean posts, 85% are covered by nonpolitical news falling into one of the three categories: "Korean society," "Korea news," and "offline activity". However, when there are sensitive issues occurring such as Korea's THAAD plan, anti-Korea sentiments were strongly expressed on the embassy's Weibo page, which will be discussed in the Sect. 2 of this chapter.

Comparing with Korea, France, the UK, the posts of the US embassy are much more engaged in delivering "hard" political messages, especially those with potentially high social impact for the Chinese people. The embassy generally avoids topics that might be construed as a direct criticism of Chinese authorities, and its posts usually cover aspects of US history, landscape, culture, tradition, or domestic policy. Around one-third of them fall, for instance, under the rubric of "US news," which, quite differently from 'Korea news', mainly talks about US policies, bilateral ties, and high-level exchanges. At the same time, the embassy does not shy away from commenting on some controversial issues. For example, when Chinese people expressed frustration about the level of air pollution in China, a post about the level of air pollution in Salt Lake City (PM 2.5) appeared on the US embassy's Weibo homepage. This post was commented on and reposted more than 4000 times.

In a similar fashion, responding to public concerns about soaring housing prices in Chinese large cities, the US account posted several messages talking about how much it would cost to buy a house in America. Another third of US Weibo posts were mainly service-oriented or offline-activity promotion, targeting a broader community. The importance that US attaches to its relationship with China is illustrated by the embassy's posts on two occasions: four greeting messages from President Obama, Ambassador Locke, State Secretary Kerry and the embassy during the Lunar New Year, and one post on the prospects of a bilateral relationship after Xi was elected president of China. A survey of the reposts and comments written in reaction to these entries indicates these messages were well received by Chinese Weibo users.

6.4.2   Presence-Expansion

While agenda-setting helps measure the influence from the perspective of message sender, presence-expansion looks at the same issue from the perspective of message receivers. Due to privacy and technical constraints, it is rather difficult to know precisely how many times each post has been viewed by other users. Weibo statistics allow us, however, to accurately capture two important channels of presence-expansion: reposting (how many times a post is circulated among users) and commenting (whether a post generates discussion or not). For reasons of statistical relevance, we have decided to select only Weibo feeds with more than 200 reposts or comments. The propagation route of Group > 200 feeds is first examined to find out how presence is expanded. Fifteen of the most reposted or commented feeds are then chosen from each Weibo account and reclassified according to their core messages. In so doing, we seek to find out how successful presence-expansion was, that is, whether the interest of the audience converged with the agenda-setting strategy of the message senders.

For the Korean embassy account, 50 posts out of the total of 90 received over 200 reposts or comments. This translates into more than 50% ratio. The ratio for the US embassy stood at 22%. A closer look at the three rations reveals that Korean Weibo feeds generated wider discussion among followers, with a spread of about 100–500 comments or reposts. In comparison, there were two extremes in the US case. The post about Salt Lake City was, for instance, very influential, witnessing over 4000 reposts or comments. It should be noted that even if these comments and reposts did not always reflect favorable sentiments from the audience, they did help provoke discussions, and in so doing they enhanced the visibility of the message sender.

6.4.3   Conversation-Generating

While the capacity of social media to facilitate interaction between the message sender and the audience is well recognized, the mechanism that enables this interaction is not fully understood. This is a gap this section seeks to bridge. First, what distinguishes new public diplomacy from the old one is listening. On Weibo, the users you follow indicate whom you are listening to. The number of users followed by the embassy of Korea, the US embassy has reached 423 and 334, respectively (as of April 2016). Both the US embassy and the Korea embassy tend to follow public opinion leaders in China. In general, those embassies' accounts rarely follow ordinary Weibo users and prefer instead to listen to authenticated or organizational users.

Another way by which to evaluate the level of interaction between message senders and the audience is by checking whether the feeds of the former are original or reposted from other Weibo users. The results show that all 95 posts of the Korean embassy were original, 150 out of 200 posts of the US embassy were original. Among the reposted ones, 30 posts came from ordinary users asking questions about visa policy for US embassy.

To conclude, the use of social media by the embassies of the US and Korea for public diplomatic purposes was not particularly conducive to generating genuine conversations with the target audience. As our analysis shows, digital diplomacy is being primarily used as an instrument of information dissemination. At the same time, there are important differences in the way in which the embassies set the agenda of discussion and disseminate their message. The nature of the bilateral relationships between China and the two countries largely explains these differences. Korea prefers a cautious agenda-setting strategy free of political or controversial topics. Its attempt to win the Chinese public opinion appears to pay off thus far as it can be seen from the rate of positive reposts and comments in general. The US digital diplomacy, on the other hand, reflects the long-term strategic objective of the US to facilitate a peaceful rise of China. By focusing on messages reflective of its core values and institutions, the US digital diplomacy strategy aims to provide ideological support of those seeking to steer the Chinese political system into a more democratic direction.

6.5 Challenges of Using Weibo as a Public Diplomacy Tool

6.5.1 Challenges of Using Social Media as a Public Diplomacy Tool

In Renken's study, the main challenge in using social media for public diplomacy is the use of an informal channel like Facebook for the communication of public institutions like the German missions abroad. The language commonly used on Facebook is very colloquial and informal, whereas the traditional communication of the missions through press releases and their websites is rather formal and stiff. The line between informal posts and posts that are not acceptable for a public institution is fine. It is seen as "difficult for a public institution to adopt a more informal language for broader audiences" (Rio de Janeiro 2014), because there are large differences in style and writing between the normal official embassy communication and the (still official) Facebook communication. The missions are aware of the positive sides of social media communication but also see the problems that come with it as this comment by the mission in Kiev illustrates: "I see the informal character of Facebook as a limitation on what it can do to facilitate our specific kind of communication. It is useful in providing a sense of accessibility and community, like when a cultural event is announced but it is not useful in the formalized processes for providing government services to the public. I would also doubt the usefulness and possibility in engaging in longer political dialogue with individual members of the public" (2014). Furthermore, colloquial language and jokes that would make the posts less stiff are lost through feedback loops and screening of posts by the heads of the press departments. The same is true for real-time communication; in Hanoi, for instance, the content for each single post has to be screened individually by the head of the press section before it can be posted online, making fast replies impossible.

The results of the survey and content analysis show that the fear of loss of control over the content published on public profiles is present in all missions. It includes the difficulty of moderating discussions and the risk of giving critical or inappropriate commentators a stage, which is why critical topics are avoided. The missions are aware that their posts can develop a dynamic that is hard to control and that the unpredictability of users and their reactions pose a risk to the mission's communication. According to the representation in Mexico City, they have to consider this "calculated risk every single time" they post information on an official Facebook page (2014). A further concern related to the loss of control is language barriers. The employees of the missions are not always fluent in the language of their host country, while the population of the host country is often not speaking German at all. Therefore, a lot of the profiles are kept in German and the local language, in English, or only the local language (in that case the Facebook profile is updated by a local employee). This makes reacting to comments quickly and engaging in a dialog complicated. Also, critical or inappropriate comments might not be identified as such because of language barriers. The last point connected to the loss of control is the relative anonymity of users that comes with the Internet. Sometimes, users make inappropriate remarks (including e.g. racism or anti-Semitism) that can publicly be seen by other users of the missions' pages. "Very rarely people feel they need to let off steam by airing some questionable political views in their comments even though there was no connection with the original post" (Brussels 2014). This means that constant monitoring of the own Facebook profile is necessary to avoid giving users who will harm the work of the mission a public stage. One strategy to cope with offensive posts is to delete them. However, the missions are hesitant to simply delete posts, as it leads to intransparency. Therefore, only "very inappropriate comments get deleted. We prefer to offer the opportunity for free speech as long as the comments are compatible with our core values" (Hanoi 2014). The preferred options are to search a dialog in private to sort out misunderstandings or to try to engage the person who posted the inappropriate or critical remark in a public discussion. "In case of criticism we acknowledge it and present our own views" (Rio de Janeiro 2014). "If there is a misunderstanding we try to clear this up and explain what was understood wrongly" (Brussels 2014). Amongst the different coping mechanisms the strategy to search for a public discussion is certainly the best. It increases the transparency of the communication, while also giving the missions another platform to spread their messages while containing the harm being done by the critical remark.

A third challenge in the use of social media is a lack or shortage of resources. While the work and the time afforded for the maintenance of social media acknowledged most missions' work distribution plans, many also see a lack of and need for more resources allocated to social media work in order to keep up the present performance or to expand the work to either more engagement on Facebook or to incorporate other platforms like for instance Twitter into the online communication. Most missions remark that they would like to spend more time on their online activities but that they do not have the resources to do so, like the mission in Sofia: "On Facebook you have to be present constantly, but we don't get additional resources for this presence. In the future we will try to keep up the work we are doing now but it will be hard to intensify our engagement or add platforms such as twitter due to manpower constraints". There is a constant need for attention and updates, which makes social media a very time-intensive tool. Also time has to be afforded in order to "stay abreast of developments" in terms of development of technology and new means of disseminating content (Istanbul 2014).

Finally, social media do not yet provide the missions with a mass audience, which is seen as a disadvantage by many representations. The mission in Kiev remarks "social media does not yet have mass audiences, so the traditional media are far from obsolete" (2014). For targeting, the young social media is a good tool, but the missions also have to reach the older parts of the population and for this social media is not effective at the moment. Indeed, most missions see social media as an additional tool in the toolbox of public diplomacy tools that reaches a small (but growing) audience that was not reached before.

6.5.2   Challenges of Using Weibo as a Public Diplomacy Tool

Apart from the challenges listed above, in analyzing the practice of using social media as a public diplomacy tool, there were two outstanding challenges facing practitioners observed.

1. The pressure of taking a position
   The fact that Weibo has become the first choice for Chinese netizens to engage in international politics, when it comes to controversial issues, for instance, the "one China" statement, foreign embassies were forced to take a position by Chinese netizens' threats of boycotting their countries' products exporting to China. For example, on 20 January 2015, Tai Wan San Li news announced

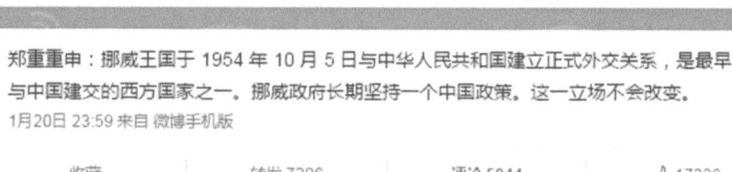

挪威驻华大使馆 V
挪威驻华大使馆官方微博

＋关注

郑重重申：挪威王国于 1954 年 10 月 5 日与中华人民共和国建立正式外交关系，是最早
与中国建交的西方国家之一。挪威政府长期坚持一个中国政策。这一立场不会改变。
1月20日 23:59 来自 微博手机版

收藏   转发 7206   评论 5944   👍 17338

Fig. 6.3 Weibo Post by Norway Embassy

that "Norway migration department acknowledges Tai Was is a country," Norway, Sweden's quick response on Weibo about "one China" statement, stated "Declaration: Norway Kingdom established diplomatic relationship with China since 5th October 1954, it is one of the Western countries that started bilateral relationship with China. Norway government has been persistent on the one China policy. This will not change". And the promise of buying more salmon fish from Norway and Ikea furniture from Sweden were then quickly made by Chinese netizens (Fig. 6.3).

2. The place for political protest

What has also been observed is that, although embassies like Korea, Japan, tried to limit their daily post to nonpolitical topics, when it comes to sensitive and controversial issues, their Weibo accounts became an ideal place for Chinese Weibo users to lodge their protests and leave protesting comments. In other words, foreign embassies Weibo pages are used as a political protesting platform by Chinese netizens. For instance, the President of Korea Park announced the THAAD deployment to South Korea on 9 July 2016, soon after the news spread out, Chinese netizens quickly got onto Korean embassy's Weibo page, and left heavy comments to condemn this action.

6.6   CONCLUSION

The trend of opening a social media account and assuming that dialog and exchange will happen just because one is "online" is a very common phenomenon today (Renken 2014). Social media are being celebrated for being the solution to communication problems, because of their ability to create dialog, because vast audiences can be reached with just one click, and because messages will reach these audiences at the blink of an eye. In comparison with more conventional means of communication, social media does present three key advantages for conducting public diplomacy. It offers a highly effective instrument for delivering information, it makes possible for the intended message to reach deep into the target audience, and it enables a two-way conversation between diplomats and the foreign public. However, the analysis shows that digital diplomacy is being primarily used as an instrument of information dissemination and much less for engaging the audience in a two-way dialog. It is apparent that certain interactive features of social media are still present, such as the comments and reposts, which enable embassies to learn about the opinions of their audience and readjust their tactics and strategies accordingly. The nature of the bilateral relationship between countries also influences the way in which social media is being used for diplomatic purposes.

However, it is found that, social media does not create dialog, it provides a platform to have a dialog, but someone has to be engaged in the dialog. This includes not only the organization wanting to send out a message but also the required audience. In the case of foreign embassies' Weibo accounts, even though embassies try to avoid political topics, engagement in political issues by Chinese netizens is inevitable. PD practitioners still have to realize that in order to have a dialog they have to send a message that is of actual interest to their audience and that they have to find the right audience for their messages (Renken 2014). Just because it is easier today to reach a lot of people does not mean that these people will be listening to what one has to say. Next chapter will set the discussion within Grunig's theory.

References

Amt, A (2013). 17. *Bericht der bundesregierung—auswärtige kultur—und bildungspolitik*. Retrieved 03/06, 2014, from https://www.auswaertige-samt.de/cae/servlet/contentblob/670488/publicationFile/189745/AKBP-Bericht_2012-2013.pdf.

Bjola, C., & Jiang, L. (2015). Social media and public diplomacy, in Bjola & Holmes (Eds.), *Digital diplomacy: Theory and practice*. Routledge: New York.

Bjola, C., & Jiang, L. (2015). Social media and public diplomacy in Bjola & Holmes (Eds.), *Digital diplomacy: Theory and practice*. pp. 71–87. London: Routledge.

Brussels. (2014). Answers to the questionnaire "social media use in public diplomacy" by the mission in Brussels. Survey results "social media use in public diplomacy".

Cull, N. J. (2009). Public diplomacy: Lessons from the past. CPD perspectives on public diplomacy, paper 2. Los Angeles, CA: USC Center on Public Diplomacy.

Cull, N. (2012). *The long road to public diplomacy 2.0: The internet in U.S. Public diplomacy*. Paper presented at the workshop International Relationships in the Information Age, April 1, 2012, International Studies Association.

Dhaka. (2014). Answers to the questionnaire "social media use in public diplomacy" by the mission in Dhaka. Survey results "social media use in public diplomacy".

Fitzpatrick, K. (2007). Advancing the new public diplomacy: A public relations perspective. *The Hague Journal of Diplomacy, 2*(3), 187–211.

Fowler, F. J. (2009). Survey research methods. London: Sage Publications.

Gilboa, E. (2000). Mass communication and diplomacy: A theoretical framework. *Communication Theory, 10*, 275–309.

Gilboa, E. (2008). Searching for a theory of public diplomacy. *Annals of the American Academy of Political and Social Science, 616*, 55–77.

Grunig, J. E., & Huang, Y.-H. (2000). From organizational effectiveness to relationship indicators: Antecedents of relationships, public relations strategies, and relationship outcomes. In J. A. Ledingham & S. D. Bruning (Eds.), *Public relations as relationship management: A relational approach to the study and practice of public relations* (pp. 23–53). Mahwah, NJ: Erlbaum.

Hanoi. (2014). Answers to the questionnaire "social media use in public diplomacy" by the mission in Hanoi. Survey results "social media use in public diplomacy".

Hocking, B. (2005). Rethinking the 'New' public diplomacy. In J. Melissen (Ed.), The new public diplomacy: soft power in international relations(pp. 28–43). Basinstoke: Palgrave Macmillan.

Hon, L. C., & Grunig, J. E. (1999). Guidelines for measuring relationships in public relations. Gainesville, FL: Institute for PR. Retrieved from http://www.instituteforprorg/research_single/guidelines_measuring_relationships..

Istanbul. (2014). Answers to the questionnaire "social media use in public diplomacy" by the mission in Istanbul. Survey results "social media use in public diplomacy".

Karaev, Z. (2005). Water diplomacy in Central Asia. *MiERIA, 9*(1), 63–69.

Kent, M. L., & Taylor, M. (1998). Building dialogic relationships through the world wide web. *Public Relations Review, 24*(3), 321–334.

Ki, E. J., & Hon, L. C. (2007). Testing the linkages among the organization–public relationship and attitude and behavioral intentions. *Journal of Public Relations Research, 19*(1), 1–23.

Kiev. (2014). Answers to the questionnaire "social media use in public diplomacy" by the mission in Kiev. Survey results "social media use in public diplomacy".

Lancaster, C. (2007). *Foreign aid: Diplomacy, development, domestic politics.* Chicago, IL: University of Chicago Press.

Ledingham (2003). Explicating relationship management as a general theory of public relations. *Public Relations Research, 15,* 181–198.

L'Etang, J. (1998). State propaganda and bureaucratic intelligence: The creation of public relations in 20th century Britain. *Public Relations Review, 24,* 413–441.

L'Etang, J. (2009). Public relations and diplomacy in a globalized world: An issue of public communication. *American Behavioral Scientist, 53*(4), 607–626.

L'Etang. (2008). L'Etang, J., & Pieczka, M. (Eds.). (2006). Public relations: Critical debates and contemporary practice. Mahwah, NJ: Lawrence Erlbaum Associates, Inc., Publishers.

Manheim, J. (1994). *Strategic public diplomacy and American foreign policy: The evolution of influence.* New York: Oxford University Press.

Marks, L. (1967). A blueprint for a digital schoolhouse, address to NAEB, Denver, 8 November 1967. Lyndon B. Johnson Library, Leonard Marks papers, box 21.

Marks, L. (1968, March). Speech as reprinted in *USIA World* (Vol. 1 No. 10).

Mexico City. (2014). Answers to the questionnaire "social media use in public diplomacy" by the mission in Mexico City. Survey results "social media use in public diplomacy".

Molleda, J. C. (2011). Global political public relations, public diplomacy, and corporate foreign policy. In S. Kiousis & J. Strömbäck (Eds.), *Political public relations: Principles and applications* (pp. 274–292). New York: Routledge.

Nye, J. (2005, December 29). On the Rise and Fall of American Soft Power. *New Perspective Quarterly, 22*(3).

Nye, J. S. (2008). Public diplomacy and soft power. *Annals of the American Academy of Political and Social Science, 616,* 94–109.

Renken, W. (2014). *Social media use in public diplomacy: A case study of the German missions' Facebook use.* Msc thesis in Strategic Public Relations jointly delievered by the University of Stirling, Lund University.

Rio de Janeiro. (2014). Answers to the questionnaire "social media use in public diplomacy" by the mission in Rio de Janeiro. Survey results "social media use in public diplomacy".

Schneider, C. (2003). *Diplomacy that works: "Best practices" in cultural diplomacy.* Washington, DC: Center for Arts and Culture, Georgetown University. Retrieved from http://ccges.apps01.yorku.ca/oldsite/IMG/pdf/03_Schneider.pdf.

Seib, P. (2012). Real-time diplomacy: Politics and power in the social media era. Berlin: Springer.

Signitzer, B. H., & Coombs, T. (1992). Public relations and public diplomacy: Conceptual convergences. *Public Relations Review, 18*(2), 137–147.

Signitzer, B., & Wasmer, C. (2006). Public diplomacy: A specific governmental public relations function. In C. Botan & V. Hazleton (Eds.), *Public relations theory II* (pp. 435–464). Mahwah, NJ: Lawrence Erlbaum.

Snow, N. (2008). International exchanges and the U.S. image. *Annals of the American Academy of Political and Social Science, 616,* 198–221.

Stein, J. (Ed.). (2011). Diplomacy in the digital age: Essays in honour of ambassador Allan Gotlied.Canada: McClelland & Stewart.

Stockholm. (2014). *Answers to the questionnaire "social media use in public diplomacy" by the mission in Stockholm.* Survey results "social media use in public diplomacy".

Walz, A. (2014, April 8). Personal communication.

Wang, J. (2006). Managing national reputation and international relations in the global era: Public diplomacy revisited. *Public Relations Review, 32,* 91–96.

Warsaw. (2014). Answers to the questionnaire "social media use in public diplomacy" by the mission in Warsaw.Survey Results "Social edia use in public diplomacy".

Waters, R. D. (2009). Measuring stewardship in public relations: A test exploring impact on the fundraising relationship. *Public Relations Review, 35*(2), 113–119.

Waters. (2011). Squawking, tweeting, cooing, and hooting: Analyzing the communication patterns of government agencies on Twitter. *Journal of Public Affairs, 11*(4).

Wise, K. (2009). Public relations and health diplomacy. *Public Relations Review, 35,* 127–129.

Xifra, J. (2009). "Building sport countries" overseas identity and reputation: A case study of public paradiplomacy. *American Behavioral Scientist, 53*(4), 504–515.

Yun, S. (2006). Toward public relations theory-based study of public diplomacy: Testing the applicability of the excellence study. *Journal of Public Relations Research, 18*(4), 287–312.

Zhang, J., & Swartz, B. C. (2009). Toward a model of NGO media diplomacy in the internet age: Case study of Washington profile. *Public Relations Review, 35*(1), 47–55.

CHAPTER 7

Implications of the Western Use of Weibo and Global PR Theory

Abstract Implications of foreign embassies' use of Weibo and global PR theory dissects PR strategy and tactics into several dimensions and discuss them accordingly.

Keywords Grunig's PR theories · Public diplomacy · Weibo

7.1 INTRODUCTION

Chapter 2 enabled Grunig's PR theories. It initiated understanding of foreign embassies' approach in practicing public diplomacy via social media platforms on the one hand, and the challenging variables they might face on the other. It suggested that social media platforms provide an unprecedented channel for public diplomacy practitioners to face the targeting audience's nationalistic sentiments directly; therefore, it generated unprecedented issues that global PR practitioners need to be aware of. The systemic empirical data provided so far in this book has questioned the assumed effective "two-way communication," which is one of the very rare available works in academia. This chapter will critically examine Grunig's global PR theories in relation to the foreign embassies' use of Weibo.

© The Author(s) 2017
Y. Jiang, *Social Media and e-Diplomacy in China*,
DOI 10.1057/978-1-137-59358-0_7

125

7.2   SOCIAL MEDIA AND GRUNIG'S PR THEORY

Long before the term "social media" was coined, Grunig advocated a methodology of public relations that puts communicating with "publics" first, above the tactics of media relations. Until the rise of social media, the practice of public relations was too often characterized as media relations, and anyone who has worked in the field knows that it's a common misperception that PR = media relations. Grunig (1993, pp. 141–143) suggests that public diplomacy is using public relations strategies in the diplomatic communication with foreign publics. By the same token, Signitzer and Coombs argue that "public relations and public diplomacy seek similar objectives and use similar tools" (1992, p. 137). In fact, one of the major theories in public relations, the Excellence Theory by Grunig et al. (2002) has been successfully applied to public diplomacy (Gilboa 2008; Yun 2006, 2008), thus, showing that both disciplines are indeed sharing objectives and tools. The conceptual closeness between public diplomacy and public relations (l'Etang 2009; Yun 2006) makes public diplomacy an appropriate field of study for the master thesis of a public relation's major.

Research focusing on the use of social media as tools for public diplomacy is scarce. The research on social media that does exist analyzes blogs (e.g. Traynor et al. 2008), focuses heavily on the US context (e.g. Cull 2009, 2013; Zaharna 2010), or on social media tools used for other purposes than public diplomacy (e.g. Henderson and Bowley 2010; Smith 2010; Wright and Hinson 2012, 2013. For the German case, previous research is "still lacking" (Auer and Srugies 2013, p. 8). Furthermore, there is some quite extensive research on the dialogic principles/dialog, but these studies take place in fields such as public relations and not in public diplomacy (Kent and Taylor 1998, 2002).

In his 2009 paper, Paradigms of global public relations in an age of digitalization, Grunig argues that social media has the potential to make the practice of PR a more "global, strategic, two-way and interactive, symmetrical or dialogical, and socially responsible," while still calling social media a "fad."

Grunig (2009) argues in favor of two-way communication and highlights the significance social media can have on this dialogic communication. He states that social media used to its full potential can provide public relations with a more two-way and interactive, global, strategic, and socially responsible approach. However, the practice of foreign embassies' two-way communication on Weibo has illustrated the difficulties of using social media to fufill these goals. Although Grunig's global public relations theory suggests that practice in different countries should be different based on culture, political system, economic system, media system, level of economic development, and extent and nature of activism in a certain country. But elements like the existence of China's nationalistic sentiments online that pose a great obstacle in implementing a two-way systematic communication were not considered. It is arguable that a one-way communication approach might work better in some contexts in public diplomacy. The next section will dissect PR strategy and tactics into several dimensions and discuss them accordingly (Duhe, S.C., New Media and Public Relations, p. 7).

7.3   Public Relation Strategy

The rise of social media has inspired high hopes that a tool to create real dialog in the form of public diplomacy 2.0 has been found. These hopes and possibilities but also the pitfalls and risks of the dialogic 2.0 version of public diplomacy have already been addressed in public relations theory (Renken 2014). In its public relations context dialog is defined by the attempt to reach "as many stakeholders as possible," by treating the participants in the communication as persons, not merely members of a target or interest group, by not only speaking but also listening, and by creating situations in which the participants are encouraged to speak their mind (Theunissen and Noordin 2012, p. 10).

Dialog can be described as a "communicative orientation" (Kent and Taylor 2002, p. 25). According to Kent and Taylor (1998) dialogic communication is "any negotiated exchange of ideas and opinions" (p. 325). They have identified five principles of dialogic communication that can be used by organizations to facilitate open communication with their publics: ease of interface, conservation of visitors (meaning that users should be kept on the website and not be let astray by links to other pages), generation of return visits, providing useful information to a variety of publics, and maintaining a dialogical loop (Kent and Taylor 1998, pp. 326–331). They can be divided into two groups or clusters: the technical and design cluster ("ease of use, usefulness of information, and conservation of visitors") and the dialogic one ("dialogical loop and generating return visits") (Kent and Taylor 2002, p. 277).

Therefore, public relations strategy is about actions that an organization can take to accomplish its goals and objectives (Cutlip et al. 2006). On the strategic side, four public relations dimensions reflect organizational approaches to problem-solving or organizational worldviews about the management of relationships with stakeholders. These dimensions may be considered strategic in the sense that they lay the foundation for the manner in which an organization might try to achieve a public relations objective: two-way communication, symmetrical communication, ethical communication, and conserving communication. Grunig (2009) has recently applied his four models of public relations to social media. He states that social media used to its full potential can provide public relations with a more two-way and interactive, global, strategic, and socially responsible approach. Furthermore, Grunig comments in the same text on the importance of different publics. He argues that the relationship with an organization's immediate publics is what matters and that organizations do not need relationships with other publics. This is a rather controversial point, especially in regards to social media where most content is open for everyone (Phillips and Young 2009a, b). Critics of this view, such as Jensen (2001), argue that audiences that might not be seen as key publics could still be important since they might engage in discussions that consequently will affect the organization's key publics and their interests. Ihlen agrees with this point of view and argues that "people, who do not seem like stakeholders at the present, might choose to take interest in a company at a later stage" (Ihlen 2008, p. 142). One might therefore look at other academics such as Ferber et al. (2007) who suggest that social media in fact encourages a three-way model of communication since social media allows a third party to receive messages. Some might argue that there is a fear of losing control over messages when they are spread online but others claim that the advantages of broadening conversations are more important (Kanter and Fine 2010).

7.4   Two-Way Communication

James Grunig (2009) argues in favor of two-way communication and highlights the significance social media can have on this dialogic communication. Both public relations and social media are about exchanging information (Phillips and Young 2009a, b) which supports arguments from public relations practitioners proclaiming positive outcomes through the use of social media. Research on organization's use of online communication for the facilitation of dialogic communication with their stakeholders has shown that organization are using technical and design methods to reach their publics but do not use the full dialogic potential of their online tools (Bortree and Seltzer 2009; Kent et al. 2003; Park and Reber 2008; Seltzer and Mitrook 2007; Sweetser and Lariscy 2008; Taylor et al. 2001; Traynor et al. 2008). In other words social media channels are still "under-utilized by organizations to facilitate dialogic communication with stakeholders" (Rybalko and Seltzer 2010, p. 340).

Dialog has not only the potential to lead to more two-way communication; there is the potential for risk in dialogic communication as well. In their discussion of a dialog project conducted in New Zealand, Zorn, Roper, and Motion (in Heath et al. 2006, pp. 366, 367), for example, refer to increased risk and vulnerability involved when engaging in dialog. One major aspect of dialog is the unpredictability that comes with it. Because of this unpredictability the outcome of the dialog might not be in the favor of the participants. Furthermore, dialog does not only bring up similarities but also differences in the positions of the participants. Thus, it may lead to disagreement instead of agreement, thereby harming the organization or the stakeholder (Theunissen and Noordin 2012, p. 11). Leitch and Neilson (2001) agree and say that real dialog has the potential to "produce unpredictable and dangerous outcomes" and that in order to "reduce both uncertainty and the potential for damage, […] organizations may attempt to determine in advance the terms of any public debate in which they engage (p. 135). Because of the dangers that genuine dialogue poses, organizations might be less likely to engage in it" (Theunissen and Noordin 2012, p. 11). For individuals there are risks in dialog: they have to open up and share intimate details about themselves. For organizations, the risks are similar; real dialog can reveal the true identity of an organization and destroy the image it has built towards the outside and towards stakeholders. Organizations that have carefully built their public image may not participate in dialog because they fear "exposure and loss of control over their image and reputation" (Theunissen and Noordin 2012, p. 11).

A further risk when engaging in dialog with one group of stakeholders is that it might alienate another group. Taylor (in Heath et al. 2006, p. 357) gives an example of this process in citing a case in which the national police force upgraded their internal communications system. After first support the project failed five years later; while a group within the police force improved its internal communication, other groups and individuals became antagonistic and the relationships between the groups fell apart.

The direction of communication underlies one part of the initial conceptualization of the four models of public relations (Grunig 1995). Defined here, two-way communication measures whether information flows from the organization to the public and vice versa, or whether the organization puts out information without seeking any input or feedback. The empirical data collected in Chaps. 3 and 4 show that Weibo does provide a channel to maximize the possibility of two-way communication.

7.5   SYMMETRICAL COMMUNICATION

The second characteristic underlying the original four public relations models had been the purpose of communication, specifically, whether the organization was interested in changing the public only or changing both the public and itself (Grunig 1995). When an organization sought to change only its target publics, it was said to be asymmetrical, whereas symmetrical communication denoted an organization that was willing to make mutual adjustments in its relationship with stakeholders. As discussed above, the concept of symmetrical communication has generated much scholarship in public relations. The use of Weibo by foreign embassies in Beijing is considered as asymmetrical by the author, because for public diplomacy, the main task is to "change" the target publics instead of the embassies themselves. Two additional public relations dimensions reflecting organizational strategy have grown out of the concept of symmetrical communication: ethical communication and conservation.

7.6   ETHICAL COMMUNICATION

Ethical communication in essence looks at the extent to which an organization behaves with honesty, accuracy, and other ethical considerations in its public relations efforts. In some recent research, the dimensions of symmetrical and ethical public relations behaviors were collapsed, since statistical analysis showed that only one factor was extracted from the items that constructed the symmetrical and ethical dimensions. It was found that symmetrical communication is inherently the most ethical of the original models of public relations (Grunig 1996), as well as for the methodological merging of these two dimensions. Social media platforms such as Weibo are exposing foreign embassies to the whole public; therefore, this platform becomes the first battle site if any unethical communication found out by the public.

Milton Friedman argued in 1970 that businesses do not have responsibilities towards society and that their sole purpose is to make a profit (Friedman 1970). A rather controversial view that has since then been challenged by many others. They state an importance of acting ethically in order to achieve the support from society (Gallagher 2005) and to avoid bad reputation (Treviño and Nelson 2004). Although ethics are evolving because of changing times and cultures (Svensson and Wood 2003), they are to be used as guidelines in terms of value formation and decision-making within an organization (Harrison 2004). Many see ethical behavior as "the right thing to do" (Treviño and Nelson 2004, p. 23) or, like Kant, as a moral obligation (Guyer 2007) and for the public relations discipline it is a crucial aspect of being a credible function within an organization (Bowen 2004).

The most cited piece of public relations work to date is the 1984 textbook Managing Public Relations by James E. Grunig and Todd Hunt (Pasadeos et al. 2010). Grunig and Hunt established four models of public relations, which include press agentry/publicity, public information, two-way asymmetric, and two-way symmetric communication. Grunig and Hunt suggest that the two-way symmetrical model, which advocates mutual understanding and dialog, is the one to aspire towards in terms of best practice and ethics within public relations.

One of the most well-known writers on ethical public relations is Patricia Parsons (2008) who sees the public relations function as a social conscience to an organization and argues that every public relations practitioner needs to accept personal and professional responsibility and to value integrity above anything else.

Critics such as Miller and Dinan (2008) see "ethical PR" as an oxymoron and they argue that public relations is simply propaganda and "spin." Miller and Dinan are both social theorists and therefore look at corporate communication from that specific point of view whereas respected academics such as Jacquie L'Etang are criticizing from within the public relations discipline. L'Etang (2008) sees the lack of professionalism as a major issue and blames weak definitions and guidelines. These can be further developed internally within the industry but wider issues such as trust need to be gained by the public.

7.7   Conservation

Another dimension of public relations behavior that grew out of the concept of symmetrical communication—or, more specifically, asymmetrical communication—was articulated in recent scholarship as conservation (Sha and pine 2004), meaning that organizations refuse to change, that is, they conserve their own fundamental agendas. Sha and pine (2004) argued that symmetrical and asymmetrical behaviors should be viewed independently, rather than opposite ends of a single continuum, and she applied Noether's theorem from mathematical formula that proves the existence of invariance of some aspect of any physical phenomenon in the face of simultaneous change produced by that phenomenon. Thus, Sha and pine (2004) used Noether's theorem to argue that organizational changes wrought by symmetrical communication could only occur with the simultaneous maintenance of some other aspect of the organization.

Sha and pine (2004) related "conserving" public relations behaviors to what had previously been called asymmetrical behaviors or pure advocacy behaviors. Empirical support for the conceptual separation of the original symmetrical/asymmetrical dimension had appeared as early as Rhee (1999), who found that symmetrical and asymmetrical behaviors were not mutually exclusive among practitioners in South Korea. Comparing the Weibo content between US embassy and Korea embassy, it is arguable that the practice of US embassy's Weibo is conserved to some extent.

A focus on essential influencers is important (Breakenridge 2008) but interactivity where there is a two-way flow of information might be crucial since any public can become more than just a 'viewer' (Marshall 2004). Interactivity online implies stakeholder participation and contribution by publics attracted to the site unintentionally or key publics whom the organization aims to target with new online communication tools (Motion 2000). It has been argued that interactivity entails the exchange of communication and it has also been suggested that users "gain more control over the communication process in interactive communication" (Quiring 2009, p. 901). Furthermore, there are possibilities for companies to come across as more human when communicating online through channels such as blogs (Scoble and Israel 2006) but in order for this to occur it is essential that organizations maintain a high level of authenticity through real people discussing real issues (Kanter and Fine 2010).

7.8   PUBLIC RELATIONS TACTICS

Public relations tactics are about concrete ways in which organizations might execute or support their strategies (Cutlip et al. 2006; Wilson and Ogden 2004). On the tactical side, three dimensions reflect actual ways in which public relations strategies might be executed: that is, through mediated communication, interpersonal communication, or social activities (Duhe 2007).

7.8.1   *Mediated communication*

The concept of mediated communication examines public relations behaviors that occur through some kind of mass media technology, such as the Internet or broadcast television. Because this dimension offers a concrete way of doing public relations activities, mediated communication is considered tactical in nature. Although Grunig (2001) placed mediated and interpersonal communication as two ends of the same dimension, other scholars (e.g., Huang 1997; Rhee 1999; Sha 1999b) believed that separating the interpersonal/mediated dimension was more appropriate. Measuring mediated communication and interpersonal communication separately meant that organizations were no longer viewed as expressing one behavior at the expense of the other, which seems particularly relevant given the growth of new media technologies being used in public relations today.

The separation of the interpersonal/mediated dimension proved to be useful in explaining the communicative behaviors of the Democratic Progressive Party on Taiwan, which showed high levels of both interpersonal and mediated public relations behaviors (Sha 1999a, b). These findings also underscored the importance of interpersonal relationships in public relations practice, perhaps first articulated by Sriramesh (1992) and reinforced by subsequent scholarship (e.g., Jo and Kim 2004; Shin et al. 2002). The use of separate scales to measure interpersonal communication and mediated communication was reinforced in Grunig et al. (2002).

7.8.2   *Interpersonal communication*

This tactical dimension of public relations centers on activities that take place either face-to-face or through one-on-one communication, such as via the telephone. Given the explosion in personal media technologies, however, much more research needs to be done on the tactical dimensions of public relations to determine whether some new activities, such as instant messaging, should be viewed as mediated or interpersonal communication (Duhe 2007).

7.8.3   *Social activities*

This tactical dimension of public relations looks at a special kind of interpersonal communication—activities that take place in a social context, but with a view toward accomplishing public relations objectives. Some examples of social activities might include banquet or gift-giving exchanges. The emphasis of this public relations dimension is on the opportunity to cultivate one-on-one, interpersonal relationships between organizational representatives and stakeholders; thus, large, impersonal special events, such as a rock concert, would not be considered reflective of this dimension.

The concept of social activities was offered by Huang (2001) and grew out of her work in Asia showing the importance of social activities in the maintenance of organizational relationships. Specifically, Huang argued that social connections (called guanxi in Chinese), the cultivation of connections (la guanxi), and the strategic use of connections (gao guanxi) were essential elements of public relations practice that differed from simple behaviors or strategies of interpersonal communication. A second aspect of social activities lies in the Chinese term renqing, which involves both maintaining and being supportive of one's social contacts. To measure this dimension, Huang (1997) extracted several of the items originally used to measure interpersonal communication.

7.9   Conclusion

The academic research on the potential of social media has mainly been developed during the last decade of rapid growth in Internet use (Grunig 2009). However, Kent and Taylor established the potential of relationship building via the web as early as 1998 when they discussed the value of the web as a "dialogic communication medium" (1998, p. 331). They also made a valuable point stressing that technology itself will not create these relationships; instead it is how it is used that will decide on the outcome.

Trust and transparency is increasingly important for organizations in order to build relationships and create support (Coombs and Holladay 2010) and ethical aspects of public relations are vital in terms of the discipline's credibility within an organization (Bowen 2004). James Grunig (2009) argues in favor of two-way communication and highlights the significance social media can have on this dialogic communication. Both public relations and social media are about exchanging information (Phillips and Young 2009a, b) which supports arguments from public relations practitioners proclaiming positive outcomes through the use of social media.

These new dimensions change the conventional way of thinking about public relations practice as being one of four traditional models: press agentry, public information, two-way asymmetrical, and two-way symmetrical. Given the increasing complexity of public relations practice, compounded by new media technologies and global ramifications for organizational actions, thinking about public relations activities as strategic and tactical dimensions helps us to understand how a research-based practice of public relations can contribute to organizational effectiveness in the strategic planning process of our field. These new dimensions of public relations also offer a more complex way to measure organizational relationships with stakeholders across space, time, and new media, thus enabling more sophisticated organizational efforts in the research and evaluation phases of the four-step process.

REFERENCES

Auer, C., & Srugies, A. (2013). Public diplomacy in Germany. CPD. Perspectives on public diplomacy, paper 5. Los Angeles, CA: USC Center on Public Diplomacy.

Bortree, D. S., & Seltzer, T. (2009). Dialogic strategies and outcomes: An analysis of environmental advocacy groups' Facebook profiles. *Public Relations Review, 35*, 317–319.

Bowen, S. A. (2004). Expansion of ethics as the tenth generic principle of public relations excellence: A Kantian theory and model for managing ethical issues. *Journal of Public Relations Research, 16*(1), 65–92.

Breakenridge, D. (2008) PR 2.0: New media, new tools, new audiences. Upper Saddle River, NJ: Pearson Education.

Coombs, W. T., & Holladay, S. J. (2010). *PR strategy and application: Managing influence.* West Sussex, UK: Wiley.

Cull, N. J. (2009). Public diplomacy: Lessons from the past. CPD perspectives on public diplomacy, paper 2. Los Angeles, CA: USC Center on Public Diplomacy.

Cull, J. (2013). The long road to public diplomacy 2.0: The internet in US public diplomacy. *International Studies Review, 15*(1), 123–139.

Cutlip, S. M., Center, A. H., & Broom, G. M. (2006). *Effective public relations* (9th ed.). Upper Saddle River: Prentice Hall.

Duhe, S. C. (Ed.) 2007. *New Media and Public Relations.* New York: Peter Lang.

Ferber, P., Foltz, F., & Pugliese, R. (2007). Cyberdemocracy and online politics: A new model of interactivity. *Bulletin of Sciency, Technology & Society, 27*(5), 391–400.

Friedman, M. (1970). *The social responsibility of business is to increase its profits.* Retrieved January 23, 2011, from http://www.colorado.edu/student-groups/libertarians/issues/friedman-soc-resp-business.html.

Gallagher, S. (2005). A strategic response to Friedman's critique of business ethics. *Journal of Business Strategy, 26*(6), 55–60.

Gilboa, E. (2008). Searching for a theory of public diplomacy. *Annals of the American Academy of Political and Social Science, 616,* 55–77.

Grunig, J. E. (1993). Public relations and international affairs: Effects, ethics and responsibility. *Journal of International Affairs, 47*(1), 137–162.

Grunig, J. E. (1995). The Theoretical Basis of Public Relations. In D. Swanston & R. Kendall (Eds.), *Accreditation sourcebook* (pp. 37–52). New York: Public Relations Society of America.

Grunig, J. E. (2001). Two-way symmetrical public relations: Past, present, and future. In R. L. Heath (Ed.),*Handbook of public relations* (pp. 11–30). Thousand Oaks, CA: Sage.

Grunig, J. E. (2009). Paradigms of global public relations in an age of digitalisation. *Prism, 6*(2). http://praxis.massey.ac.nz/prism_on-line_journ.html.

Grunig, J. E., Grunig, L. A., & Dozier, D. M. (1996). Das situative model exzellenter public relations: Schlussfolgerungen aus einer internationalen studie (The contingency model of excellent public relations: Conclusions from an international study). In G. Bentele, H. Steinmann, & A. Zerfass (Eds.), *Dialogorientierte unternehmenskommunikation (Dialogue-oriented approaches to communication)* (pp. 199–228). Berlin: Vistas.

Grunig, L. A., Grunig, J. E., & Dozier, D. M. (2002). *Excellent public relations and effective organizations: A study of communication management in three countries.* Mahwah, NJ: Lawrence Erlbaum.

Guyer, P. (2007). *Kant's groundwork for the metaphysics of morals.* London: Continuum International Publishing Group.

Harrison, J. (2004). Conflicts of duty and the virtues of Aristotle in public relations ethics: Continuing the conversation commenced by Monica Walle. *PRism 2.* Retrieved January 28, 2017, from http://praxis.massey.ac.nz/fileadmin/Praxis/Files/Journal_Files/Issue2/Harrison.pdf.

Heath, R. L., Pearce, W. B., Shotter, J., Taylor, J. R., Kersten, A., Zorn, T., et al. (2006). The processes of dialogue: Participation and legitimation. *Management Communication Quarterly, 19*(3), 341–375.

Henderson, A., & Bowley, R. (2010). Authentic dialogue? The role of "friendship" in a social media recruitment campaign. *Journal of Communication Management, 14*(3), 237–257.

Huang, Y. H. (1997). *Public relations strategies, relational outcomes, and conflict management strategies.* Unpublished doctoral dissertation, University of Maryland, College Park.

Huang, Y. - H. (2001). OPRA: A cross cultural, multiple-item scale for measuring organization-public relationships. *Journal of Public Relations Research, 13*(1), 61–69.

Ihlen. (2008). Mapping the environment for corporate social responsibility: Stakeholders, publics and the public sphere. *Corporate Communications: An International Journal, 13*(2), 135–146.

Jensen, I. (2001). Public relations and emerging functions of the public sphere: An analytical framework. *Journal of Communication Management, 6*(2), 133–147.

Jo, S., & Kim, Y. (2004). Media or personal relations? Exploring media relations dimensions in South Korea. *Journalism and Mass Communication Quarterly, 81*(2), 292–306.

Kanter, B., & Fine, A. H. (2010). *The networked nonprofit.* San Fransisco, CA: Wiley.

Kent, M. L., & Taylor, M. (1998). Building dialogic relationships through the world wide web. *Public Relations Review, 24*(3), 321–334.

Kent, M. L., & Taylor, M. (2002). Toward a dialogic theory of public relations. *Public Relations Review, 28*(1), 21–37.

Kent, M. L., Taylor, M., & White, W. J. (2003). The relationship between Web site design and organizationalresponsiveness to stakeholders. *Public Relations Review, 29*(1), 63–77.

L'Etang. (2008). L'Etang, J. & Pieczka, M. (Eds.), (2006). Public relations: Critical debates and contemporary practice. Mahwah, NJ: Lawrence Erlbaum Associates.

L'Etang, J. (2009). Public relations and diplomacy in a globalized world: An issue of public communication. *American Behavioral Scientist, 53*(4), 607–626.

Leitch, S., & Neilson, D. (2001). Bringing publics into public relations: new theoretical frameworks for practice. In R. Heath & G. Vasquez (Eds.), *Handbook of public relations* (pp. 127–138).Thousand Oaks: Sage.

Marshall, P. D. (2004). *New media cultures.* London: Arnold Publishers.

Miller, D., & Dinan, W. (2008). *A century of spin: How public relations became the cutting edge of corporate power.* London: Pluto Press.

Motion, J. (2000). Electronic relationships: Interactivity, internet branding and the public sphere. *Journal of Communication Management, 5*(3), 217–230.

Park, H., & Reber, B. (2008). Relationship building and the use of websites: How fortune 500 companies use their websites to build relationships. *Public Relations Review*, 39(4), 409–411.

Parsons, P. (2008). *Ethics in Public Relations* (2nd ed.). Kogan Page Limited: UK.

Pasadeos, Y., Berger, B., & Renfro, B. (2010). Public relations as a maturing discipline: An update on research networks. *Journal of Public Relations Research*, 22(2), 136–158. doi:10.1080/10627261003601390.

Phillips, D., & Young, P. (2009a). *Online public relations: A practical guide to developing an online strategy in the world of social media*. London: Kogan Page.

Phillips, D., & Young, P. (2009b). *Online public relations: A practical guide to developing an online strategy in the world of social media* (2nd ed.). London: Kogan Page Limited.

Quiring, O. (2009). What do users associate with 'interactivity'? A qualitative study on user schemata. *New Media Society*, 11(6), 899–920.

Renken, W. (2014). Social media use in public diplomacy: A case study of the German missions' facebook use. Msc thesis in strategic public relations jointly delievered by the University of Stirling and Lund University.

Rhee, Y. (1999). *Confucian culture and excellent public relations: A study of generic principles and specific applications in South Korean public relations practice*.Unpublish master's dissertation. University of Maryland, College Park.

Rybalko, S., & Seltzer, T. (2010). Dialogic communication in 140 characters or less: How fortune 500 companies engage stakeholders using twitter. *Public Relations Review*, 36(4), 336–341.

Scoble, R., & Israel, S. (2006). *Naked conversations: How blogs are changing the way businesses talk with customers*. Hoboken, N.J: Wiley.

Seltzer, T., & Mitrook, M. (2007). The dialogic potential of weblogs in relationships building. *Public Relations Review*, 33(2), 227–229.

Sha, B. L. (1999a). *Cultural public relations: identity, activism, globalization and gender in the Democratic Party on Taiwan*. Unpublished PHD dissertation, University of Maryland, College Park.

Sha, B. L. (1999b). Noether's Theorem: The Science of Symmetry and the Law of Conservation. *Journal of Public Relations Research*, 16(4), 319–416.

Sha, B. -L., & Pine, P. (2004, March). *Using the situational theory of publics to develop an education campaign regarding child sexual abuse*. Paper presented to the International Interdiscliplinary Public Relations Research Conference, Miami, FL, USA.

Shin, J. H., Cropp, F., & Cameron, G. T. (2002). *Asking what matters most: A national survey of PR professional response to the contingency model*. In Paper presented at the annual meeting of the Association for Education in Journalism and Mass Communication.

Signitzer, B. H., & Coombs, T. (1992). Public relations and public diplomacy: Conceptual convergences. *Public Relations Review, 18*(2), 137–147.

Smith, B. G. (2010). Socially distributing public relations: Twitter, Haiti, and interactivity in social media. *Public Relations Review, 36*(4), 329–335.

Sriramesh, K. (1992). Societal culture and public relations: Ethnographic evidence from India. *Public Relations Review, 18*(2), 201–211.

Svensson, G., & Wood, G. (2003). The dynamics of business ethics: A function of time and culture—cases and models. *Management Decision, 41*(4), 350–361.

Sweetser, K. D., & Lariscy, R. W. (2008). Candidates make good friends: An analysis of candidates' uses of facebook. *International Journal of Strategic Communication, 2*(3), 175.

Taylor, M., White, W. J., & Kent, M. L. (2001). How activist organizations are using the internet to build relationships. *Public Relations Review, 27*(3), 263–284.

Theunissen, P., & Wan Noordin, W. N. (2012). Revisiting the concept "dialogue" in public relations. *Public Relations Review, 38*(1), 5–13.

Traynor, J., Pointevit, M., Bruni, B., Stiles, H., Raines, K., & Little, H., et al. (2008). On the ballot and in the loop: The dialogic capacity of campaign blogs in the 2008 election. Paper presented at the annual meeting of the Association for Education in Journalism and Mass Communication, Chicago, IL.

Trevino, L. K., & Nelson, K. A. (2004). *Managing business ethics: Straight talk about how to do it right* (3rd ed.). Hoboken, NJ: Wiley.

Wilson, L. J., & Ogden, J. D. (2004). *Strategic communications planning: For effective public relations and marketing* (4th ed.). Dubuque, IA: Kendall/Hunt.

Wright, D., & Hinson, M. (2012). Examining how social and emerging media have been used in public relations between 2006 and 2012: A longitudinal analysis. *Public Relations Review, 6*(4), 32–56.

Wright, D., & Hinson, M. (2013). An updated examination of social and emerging media use in public relations practice: A longitudinal analysis between 2006 and 2013. *Public Relations Journal, 7*(3), 20–42.

Yun, S. (2006). Toward public relations theory-based study of public diplomacy: Testing the applicability of the excellence study. *Journal of Public Relations Research, 18*(4), 287–312.

Yun, S. (2008). Cultural consequences on excellence in public diplomacy. *Journal of Public Relations Research, 20*(2), 207–230.

Zaharna, R. (2010). Battles to bridges: US strategic communication and public diplomacy after 9/11. New York: Palgrave Macmillan.

CHAPTER 8

Conclusion/Open-Endedness

Abstract This chapter reminds the reader the backgrounds the book sits against, and reviews the major themes raised in this book as a way to conclude.

Keywords Public diplomacy 2.0 · New media · Cyber-nationalism

8.1 "PUBLIC DIPLOMACY 2.0", "NEW MEDIA 2.0", "CYBER-NATIONALISM 2.0"

This book is first of all set in the background of the "new" generation of public diplomacy, "public diplomacy 2.0", the term 'public diplomacy 2.0' describes new methods and modes of conducting diplomacy and international relations with the help of the Internet and information and communication technologies (ICTs). The term also refers to the study of the impact of these tools on contemporary diplomatic practices. Related (and interchangeable) terms include cyber diplomacy, net diplomacy, and digital diplomacy. Cull (2010) from Harvard University summarized the three key characteristics of it: the first characteristic is the capacity of the technology to facilitate the creation of relationships around social networks and on-line communities. The second characteristic is the related dependence of Public Diplomacy 2.0 on user-generated content from feedback and blog comments to complex user-generated items such as videos or mash-ups. The third characteristic is the underlying sense of

© The Author(s) 2017   141
Y. Jiang, *Social Media and e-Diplomacy in China*,
DOI 10.1057/978-1-137-59358-0_8

the technology as being fundamentally about horizontally arranged networks of exchange rather than the vertically arrange networks of distribution down which information cascaded in the 1.0 era. Cull has also pointed out that while the technology is entirely new the underlying pattern of relationships underlying the operation of Public Diplomacy 2.0 is not.

This book also sets in the background of the new presentation of Chinese nationalism enabled by new media. Loving one's motherland is not only a Chinese phenomenon, but the point I make here is that this "love for the motherland" has been largely in the presentation of supporting the central government, despite the corruptions of local government which have been exposed in a lot of cases. The other presentation of "love for the motherland" is the resistance to critical comments towards China. Before foreign embassies opened up Weibo accounts, Chinese nationalists used to express their condemnation via website or their own blogs/microblogs (Jiang 2012). The appearance of foreign embassies' Weibo accounts provided a direct channel for condemnation, particularly when controversial events happen. It is interesting that even an embassy choose not to broadcast any political topics, and even Chinese followers are engaging with the embassy in a very harmonious manner, it still becomes a target when any sensitive issues occur.

Xi's "Chinese dream," for example, emphasizes wealth, national pride, and obedience to authority. Media and schools stress the idea of patriotism, with "love of country" considered conterminous with "love of the Communist Party." Ideas such as democracy, human rights, and modernization are mentioned as well, but generally with the appendage "with Chinese characteristics," to indicate that they have been modified to fit into Communist Party (China Daily Mail 2015).

One of the illustrations to this current wave of nationalism is the national flag snapshot event called "Let's take a photo with our national flag" in 2014, initiated by an overseas Chinese student in Australia, this event was endorsed and echoed by thousands of Chinese across the world via social media Weibo. This is a campaign asking Chinese Internet users to post snapshots of them and the national flag online has gone viral ahead of the 65th anniversary of the founding of the People's Republic of China on Wednesday. Pictures posted on Weibo, a Twitter-like microblogging platform, show Chinese posing all over the world. In one, a woman stands in front of a wall painted with a national flag. In another, several police officers present their smartphones bearing the national flag as the wallpaper. One girl took a selfie in front of a computer with the national flag as the background. Soldiers have also posted pictures of themselves standing guard at China's borders. As of Monday, the campaign has become one of the hottest topics on Weibo, with more than 200 million comments.

This book is also set against the background of China's embrace of the market and the Internet, which are both fundamentally characterized by "liberalization" and "control". It is within this context that this book examines the anger from China's Generation Y towards the Western media, and problematizes the normative assumption of the implication of new media in practicing public diplomacy in China, as well as the dominant perceptions of Chinese government's role in shaping the new generation's anti-Western sentiments. This book is unified by a particular interest in understanding the challenges and issues posed by Chinese nationalists in practicing e-diplomacy on Weibo, because it indicates that the dominant assumption about social media ultimately being an ideal channel for two-way symmetrical communication might be problematic. This book sits in the background of understanding China's current wave of nationalism. The key feature of "country for the country" and "love of the Communist Party" of the current wave needs to be explained at this point.

Loving for its country is not unique, but one of the issues that poses a challenge to foreign embassies' is the ultra-nationalist sentiments towards "foreign hostile forces." In a propaganda video with slick production values that has gone viral on the Chinese Internet, Chinese nationalists warn viewers against what it says are US-led "foreign hostile forces" conspiring to foment a "colour revolution" similar to those in Ukraine, Georgia, and the Arab Spring in mainland China (Wen 2016). This 5-mins long video, amassed more than 10 million views within 24 h. The video has had particular resonance in China given the way official party rhetoric has doubled down on its invective aimed at the prominent four-day political show trial of lawyers and legal rights advocates, with the party-controlled judiciary portraying those on trial as having conspired with foreign agents to subvert the Chinese state, rather than seeking to advance rule of law in their country (Wen 2016).

This book also reveals the Chinese characteristic of social media. Social media is one of the fastest growing tools of modern public diplomacy. Social media is believed to provide the right channel to reach youth populations, which is one of the major goals of current public diplomacy efforts. There is no doubt that scholars and journalists believe that social media like Weibo could be used as an effective platform for foreign public diplomacy practitioners to promote "two-way" communications. However, the use of social media has its "Chinese characteristics," which is "brushed with nationalistic sentiments."

A reiteration is necessary here. I intend this book to offer a glimpse into exploring the challenges that the use of Chinese Weibo (and Chinese social media in general) posed for foreign embassies, and to provoke thoughts about better ways to use these or other tools. It is not intended as an argument against the use of local popular social media for public diplomacy purposes, but to encourage a critical look at its practice and encourage those employing it to better analyze it. This book doesn't deny that social media provides the right channel to reach youth populations, which is one of the major goals of current public diplomacy efforts. Weibo does give embassies a great channel to listen to and understand China's young populations' thoughts, aspirations, information seeking, and other behaviors. But when it comes to using the spaces for interaction, increased engagement, and thus furthering the goals of public diplomacy, the power of Weibo might have been overestimated.

I have reached the conclusions in this thesis through engagement with a wide range of disciplinary sources. In particular, I have used literature (both in Chinese and English) from disciplines subsumed under the titles of China Studies, Asian Studies, Internet Studies, Political Science, Sociology, and Anthropology. I have also used material obtained from primary research in Chinese cyberspace in Chaps. 3, 4, 5, 6, and 7 of this thesis. By drawing from these sources, I have sought to comprehend the effectiveness of foreign embassies' use of Weibo in China in a more socially and culturally engaged context, also to comprehend the concepts in the liberal context can be actualized in China without the state abandoning authoritarian characteristics. I now review some of the major themes as a way to conclude:

- Weibo has been used actively by a number of foreign embassies. It is evident that Weibo can be employed effectively in engaging with citizens, which is one of the goals of public diplomacy. It is difficult to measure its real effects simply by looking at the data collected. In fact, one of the important phenomena this research illustrates is that, the number of followers doesn't equal to high influence, the level of "conversational" communication doesn't indicate the success of e-diplomacy. Conversely, those negative and hostile comments left on some of the embassies' Weibo accounts show that the outcome of its public diplomacy task is unsuccessful.

- "Conversational" communication doesn't necessarily equate to the success of e-diplomacy. Having a high number of followers and high level of interaction with your audience, does not link to positive action. Defining public diplomacy (PD) as communication with foreign publics for the purpose of achieving a foreign policy objective, PD practitioners should be cognizant that information is different than influence. Based on the research findings, it was also arguable that the number of followers does not necessarily equate a strong connection with an audience. An account might have a million followers say nothing, even though a post gets retweeted 1000 times per day, it doesn't indicate whether those followers are supporting or against the user's communication goals.
- Nationalistic sentiments from Chinese netizens posted on US embassy's Weibo pages pose a real challenge to Weibo diplomacy. Those large amount of negative comments have a great impact on US embassy's public image.

8.2   FUTURE RESEARCH

Future research can look at the use of another popular social media platform in China—Wechat—by foreign embassies. Due to the different nature of Wechat, a couple of aspects might be worth comparing: (1) Are those five embassies also the most active ones on Wechat? (2) Does Wechat pose less challenges than Weibo for foreign embassies in China? This book aims to provoke thoughts about better ways to use these social media or other tools for public diplomacy practioners. It is not intended as an argument against the use of local popular social media for public diplomacy purposes, but to encourage a critical look at its practice and encourage those employing it to better analyze it.

In this book, without denying the usefulness of local popular social media for public diplomacy purposes, it encourages a critical look at its practice and encourage those employing it to better analyze it. This book doesn't deny that social media provides the right channel to reach youth populations, which is one of the major goals of current public diplomacy efforts. Weibo does give embassies a great channel to listen to and understand China's young populations' thoughts, aspirations, information seeking and other behaviors. But when it comes to using the spaces for interaction, increased engagement, and thus furthering the goals of public diplomacy, the power of Weibo might have been overestimated.

At the same time, future research may focus on three other areas which, I believe, are under-researched and deserve critical attention. They are: (1) the clash between Western media protocols and Chinese media protocols that has existed from the origin of the mass media in different regions and still exists in the globalized world; (2) the political participation in Chinese cyberspace that is still in its infancy; (3) the widening division and exclusion between the netizens and non-netizens in contemporary China, which is also an important factor in examining the influence of Internet media in China.

REFERENCES

China Daily Mail. (2015, May 4). *What it means to be Chinese—Nationalism and identity in Xi's China.* Retrieved August 23, 2016, from https://chinadailymail.com/2015/05/04/what-it-means-to-be-chinese-nationalism-and-identity-in-xis-china/.

Cull, N. J. (2010). Public diplomacy: Seven lessons for its future from its past. *Place branding and public diplomacy* (Vol.6, Iss. 1, pp. 11–17).

Jiang. (2012). Cyber-nationalism in China: Challenging western media's portrayal of China's censorship. Adelaide: University of Adelaide Press.

Wen, P. (2016, August 4) The Australian connection behind China's ultra-nationalist viral video. *Sydney Morning Herald.* http://www.smh.com.au/world/the-australian-connection-behind-chinas-ultranationalist-viral-video-20160803-gqkiki.html.

Bibliography

China Economic Net. (2012). Australian companies registered Weibo accounts for business opportunities. *China Economics Net*. Retrieved from http://intl. ce.cn/specials/zxgjzh/201203/30/t20120330_23202373.shtml.

Duhe, S. C. *New Media and Public Relations*. New York: Peter Lang.

Goldkorn, J. (2006c, April 27). Danwei TV 7: Muzi Mei sex blogger. Retrieved April 23, 2016, from http://www.danwei.org/danwei_tv/danwei_tv_7_mu_zimei_interview.php.

Grunig, J. E. (2003). Constructing public relations theory and practice. In B. Dervin, S. H. Chaffee & L. Foreman-Wernet (Eds.), *Communication, a different kind of horserace: Essays honoring Richard F. Carter* (pp. 85–115). Cresskill, NJ: Hampton Press.

Lawrence, P. R., & Lorsch, J. W. (1967). Organization and environment: Managing differentiation and integration: Division of Research. Boston: Harvard Business School Press.

Mackinnon, R (2009a, February 2). China's censorship 2.0: How companies censor bloggers. *First Monday, 14*(2). Retrieved June 23, 2009, from <http://firstmonday.org/htbin/cgiwrap/bin/ojs/index.php/fm/article/view/2378/2089>.

© The Editor(s) (if applicable) and The Author(s) 2017
Y. Jiang, *Social Media and e-Diplomacy in China*,
DOI 10.1057/978-1-137-59358-0